WRITING THE PAST

THE EAGLES AND DRAGONS PUBLISHING
GUIDE TO RESEARCHING, WRITING,
PUBLISHING AND MARKETING HISTORICAL
FICTION AND HISTORICAL FANTASY

ADAM ALEXANDER HAVIARAS

Writing the Past: The Eagles and Dragons Publishing Guide to Researching, Writing, Publishing and Marketing Historical Fiction and Historical Fantasy and *Eagles and Dragons Publishing Guides*

Copyright © 2019 by Adam Alexander Haviaras and Eagles and Dragons Publishing

Eagles and Dragons Publishing, Toronto, Ontario, Canada

All Rights Reserved.

The use of any part of this publication, with the exception of short excerpts for the purposes of book reviews, without the written consent of the author is an infringement of copyright law.

ISBN: 978-1-988309-35-4

First Paperback Edition

Cover designed by LLPix Designs

*Please note: There is a list of helpful resources for researching, writing, publishing, and marketing, at the back of this book.

Subscribe today!

Join the Eagles and Dragons Publishing Masters of Historical Fiction and Historical Fantasy mailing list today and get a FREE PDF of the Historical Novel Book Launch Strategy Blueprint.

Subscribers get first access to new releases, author training, special offers,
and much more.

Visit:

https://eaglesanddragonspublishing.com/eagles-and-dragons-publishing-masters-of-historical-fiction-and-historical-fantasy/

WRITING THE PAST

The Eagles and Dragons Publishing Guide to
Researching, Writing, Publishing and Marketing
Historical Fiction and Historical Fantasy

By: Adam Alexander Haviaras

PREFACE

Does the world really need another book on writing and publishing? There are so many to chose from already! But the world of publishing has changed dramatically in the last decade, and authors in various genres now have a dizzying array of publishing options and advice before them. Some groups of authors, however, have very few genre-specific resources at their disposal, particularly authors of historical fiction and historical fantasy.

Historical novelists find themselves in an interesting place today, caught between the traditional publishing world in which they have always been solidly encamped, and the new and exciting opportunities now presented to them by the world of independent publishing.

With so much choice, it truly is the best time to be an author, but like Alexander the Great setting out for the conquest of the East, those first steps can be daunting, the battles you will fight along the way numerous. The goal of this book is to try to encourage and arm aspiring and veteran historical novelists for the journey ahead with information and advice that is evergreen in the face of change.

Why did I decide to write this book now, and what makes me qualified to do so?

I've been studying history and writing historical fiction and historical fantasy for over thirty years now, and to this day I absolutely love both. Indeed, one did not come before the other, for when I fell in love with history, I immediately turned to writing fiction as the obvious way to express that love. For me, the two went together from the very beginning. Then, ten years ago, in 2009, after hearing a speaker from a Google think tank talk about the power of blogging, I decided to launch the *Writing the Past* blog as a way to connect with fellow history and historical fiction lovers around the world. The blog was a way not only to share my passion for history and archaeology, but also to share my research for my novels, two of which had already been written by that point in time.

It has been a long road to this point, but after developing a large following, writing and publishing over fifteen novels, making a good income, and founding a publishing company that I can be proud of, I thought it would be a good time to share all that I have learned with my fellow historical novelists.

It is my hope that everyone who is interested in researching, writing, publishing and marketing historical fiction and historical fantasy will be guaranteed to get at least one useful, actionable tip from the following pages that will aid them in achieving their goals.

Good luck, and may the gods smile on your endeavours!

Adam Alexander Haviaras
somewhere in the Peloponnese, 2019

PART I

RESEARCH

INTRODUCTION

What is the difference between 'historical fiction' and 'historical fantasy'? The first is fiction that is firmly set in a documented historical period and adheres strictly to the events and known ways of that period. The latter is based on, or inspired by, a particular historical period, but which has a preponderance of fantasy elements like gods and goddesses, mythological beasts and other elements that our ancient ancestors believed in, but which today have been relegated to the world of the imagination.

When it comes to research, however, there is very little difference between the two types of historical novel. The methodologies are the same as research is crucial for any historical novelist because it anchors your story in a particular period, thus transporting the reader to another time and place and giving them the escape they are in search of.

In this first section on research, you will learn about simple methodologies for historical research that do not require academic, university-level training or resources, as well as other reliable ways to gather information in preparation for writing the historical novel that you envision.

1

Be Passionate

WHEN DECIDING UPON A PARTICULAR PERIOD OR historical subject to base your book around, pick something that you are passionate about. The history behind your novel and the characters therein are crucial to connecting with your readers.

Don't look at the market to decide what to write about. Rather, pick a period of history that you truly love and are willing to immerse yourself in for a long time, and your passion for it will draw readers in like a statue at the heart of a temple.

2

Academic Study

THIS BOOK IS NOT GEARED TOWARD ACADEMICS OR people with academic training. However, the work done by academics in your particular field will be useful in the research you do, for they have laid the groundwork for knowledge.

That said, today, most of the information you need will likely be available online. You do not need to pay for university to write historical novels, unless you want to also be an academic yourself.

You want to be an author, right? So, where do you

go for the information you need to bring your historical novel to life?

3

Starting Point

IF YOU ARE AN AUTHOR WHO GENERALLY KNOWS THAT you would like to write a historical novel but are not sure of the setting or period of your novel, then you need to decide at the outset on your specific period of history.

This may seem odd to some, but I have been asked before by authors who want to write a book what period they should write about. Perhaps this is because they love history in general and the thought of writing in any period is appealing? Perhaps they want to write about what is popular at the moment in order to achieve commercial success?

Whatever the reason, it comes down to passion again. Which period of history are you most passionate about? This is important because you are going to be eating, breathing and sleeping this period of history, especially if you are planning on writing a series of books.

Do you want to set your novel in twelfth century Medieval Europe during the Crusades, or do you want your story to take place in the world of ancient Rome during the reign of Emperor Tiberius? Perhaps you have a story in mind that is set in feudal Japan and the age of the Samurai?

If you can narrow it down to a specific event, or set of events, then that is even better, as history will be the timeline for your novel and the characters within.

Think about which period, cultural group and historical events you want your novel to revolve around or be modelled on, and then go from there.

4

Time to Read!

ONCE YOU HAVE DECIDED ON A HISTORICAL SETTING and subject matter for your novel, it is time to start reading.

Find all the books you can on your period and historical events, aspects of life in that age etc., and start reading as much as you can. Immerse yourself in that world, and get to know the people and their ways until that world becomes so familiar to you that it is second nature.

This will make the actual writing easier because when you think of the history in your story, you will see and smell the land, the objects, the food - everything. If you can do this, then your writing will go much more smoothly and you can focus on your story because you won't be stopping all the time to look something up.

Depending on your personal style, you can either take copious amounts of notes, or just fill your head.

Read as much as you can and absorb everything that is useful.

5

Time to Watch!

In addition to reading, a superb way to get stuck into the world of your chosen period of history is to watch movies, television series, or documentaries and docudramas about it. If books teach you a lot, and pictures are worth a thousand words, then films and videos are worth a million.

Of course, not every period of history is represented in film, but if it is, even a little bit, then it is worth checking out. Even such things as seeing a medieval village setting in film can give you ideas for your novel, even though it may not be the exact period for your own book.

Something else to keep in mind when it comes to film…

You will hear a lot of people, especially academics, criticize historical films for their inaccuracy. My advice for this is to ignore them. It is true that many films may not be historically accurate in their mode of dress or weapons etc., but we need to remember as storytellers that film is a very different medium and not every detail can be incorporated into two hours. The filmmakers are trying to tell a story, and that must come first. Watch them, learn from them, and then fill in the gaps and inaccuracies with all that you have learned from your extensive reading.

Historical films are a good thing because they generate interest in a particular historical period, and in history in general. For example, when *Gladiator* came out, it was criticized by historians for its inaccuracies. Someone even told me that 'Romans didn't fight like that!' when referring to the opening scene. That may be true, but *Gladiator* was a brilliant film with an excellent story, and Classics enrolment in universities around the world shot through the roof following the film's release because people were interested. That's a good thing!

Watch as much as you can, as the images will fill your head and you will get ideas for your novel.

6

Where else to go for Information

THE BIG BOX AND ONLINE BOOKSTORES ARE NOT THE only places where you can go to get reading materials while doing research for your novel. Unlike the great library of Alexandria, which attempted to gather all sources in one place, the opportunities for us to find things are myriad, and some of them may surprise you.

In the next few chapters, we will go over some other sources of information that will give your novel an edge over others.

It is time to think outside the box!

7

Primary Sources

PRIMARY SOURCES ARE ONE OF THE MOST IMPORTANT and crucial elements of your research. They are sources from the period itself, from the mouths of the people of the past. For example, if you are writing about the Roman conquest of Gaul, then you would be remiss if you did not read and make use of the details in Julius Caesar's firsthand account of the campaign. Or if you are writing about the Tudors, you should certainly check out the letters between Henry VIII and Anne Boleyn, for instance, to get inside their heads.

Of course, not everything from the past has survived, but if you are fortunate enough to be writing about a period for which there are primary sources available, then you should definitely use them.

One thing to bear in mind is that even primary sources may not accurately portray historical events. Ancient and medieval writers, for example, were prone to exaggeration when it came to troop or casualty numbers in their accounts. Also, it must be remembered that history was, more often than not, written by the victors in a confrontation. I'm sure that Vercingetorix, if he had had the opportunity to write his memoirs in his prison in Rome, would have had a much different account from Caesar's of the Roman conquest of his homeland.

If you are worried about not being able to read these texts, don't be. Most primary sources have been translated from their original language into English and are available for an affordable price in such series as Penguin Classics and others.

The bottom line is, use any primary sources from your chosen period, for they will give you crucial insight into that world and the people in it.

. . .

Tip: Excellent translations of various sources are available online for free on sites such as:

- www.perseus.tufts.edu
- www.theoi.com
- www.gutenberg.org
- www.loebclassics.com (fee based)

8

Antiquarian Books

SOMETIMES, YOU NEED TO GO OLD SCHOOL FOR resources, and early historians or 'antiquarians' can be a marvellous source of information.

It is important to note that not all primary and secondary (written in the modern era) source materials have been digitized. This does not mean they are not important or useful. There are myriad sources from thousands of years of human history, and digitization projects have only really begun in earnest in the last two decades.

If you are a bookwork, then you will relish the

task of going in search of secondary sources such as antiquarian historians. These may not have the latest theories about various historical subjects or discoveries, but they can still be very useful, and often they will contain engravings or plates that bring a historical setting to life for you.

To find these books, check out used books shops, search online, or head to your public library where they can get the item you are looking for on loan from another library if they do not have it on site.

Some used and rare bookstores tend to be depositories for estate sales, and I have found many wonderful editions at such places as John K. King Used and Rare Books in Detroit, Michigan. Many of these used and rare book dealers have websites now where you can request a search for particular books, so don't forget to check them out. You never know what treasures you will find!

Tip: If you are not sure what to look for, remember to check the bibliographies of your favourite history books for titles by subject matter experts past and present.

9

Databases and Academic Papers

WHEN IT COMES TO THE LATEST, CUTTING EDGE research in a particular field of study for history, or finding articles on an obscure subject, academic papers published in journals can be some of your best secondary source materials. These are found in databases at most universities.

One example that I have made extensive use of is the International Medieval Bibliography (IMB) out of the University of Leeds. This database has articles published from 1967 to the present on almost any subject matter related to Medieval history. Find out which databases there are for your area of study and then start searching for articles.

However, you don't need to be part of Aristotle's entourage at a university to get access to these databases. Most universities will allow the public access to their libraries for a fee. But if that is not within your budget (though the fees should be minimal), you should definitely head to your local public library and ask them if they have access to the databases you are looking for.

Public libraries are places of learning for all, and in the digital age many of them have subscriptions to extensive lists of databases. Go to the public library, tell the librarian what you are looking for, and they will be more than happy to help you find what you need. We love librarians!

10

The Internet

Not even the librarians in ancient Alexandria would have been able to conceive of a resource such as the Internet. It is, truly, a titanic fount of knowledge to which most of us have access. It is one of the reasons why it is the best time to be a writer, for it has given us access to most of the information we need at our fingertips, and provided us with unprecedented opportunities to get our books out into the world.

But the Internet can also be a double-edged sword.

There is a lot of information, and in doing your

research you will need to sift carefully for the true bits of knowledge that will enrich your novel.

When you are doing your research online, be sure to check the credentials of any author whose work you are using, whether it is a blog or book. Make sure they know what they are talking about. After all, the Romans ensured the cement they used to build their foundations was solid. Likewise, you don't want to build your literary monument on a shoddy foundation.

One of the resources most people will turn to when looking up history is Wikipedia. There are pros and cons to this resource; often the information available on a particular subject is minimal, or it requires fact-checking. In the beginning, historians and academics had stern warnings for their students about using Wikipedia as a research tool but, thankfully, it has been greatly improved in recent years. If you use Wikipedia for information, always double check that information in another source to make sure it is accurate.

Another area online where you can get some guidance for your research is in specialty and enthusiast groups on such platforms as Facebook. If you are a member of one of these groups (if not, request to join them) you can ask the group a question and most of the time someone will have an answer. For example, if you are looking for a floor plan for a particular Roman villa in rural France, or want to know what the best primary source is for the Hundred Years War, put this question to the members of your chosen group and they will help you.

By all means, use the Internet. You would be mad not to. Just do it carefully.

11

Museums

THE WORD 'MUSEUM' COMES FROM THE GREEK 'mouseio' which means 'house of the Muses'.

What better place for an author to do some research! If *art begets art*, as they say, then the museum should most certainly be on your list of places to do research and immerse yourself in the past.

Even the smallest of museums will have something to inspire you. There, you can see the past up close.

Browse the faces of the statues there for a glimpse

of the hairstyles that were trendy during a particular period. Check the beards! Those faces could be characters in your book.

What is important about museums is that you not only see the monumental relics of the rich and famous of history, but also, perhaps more importantly, get a close look at the more mundane items and details of daily life for the period. It might not sound exciting to look at things such as dishes, mirrors, or dice, but items like these can add texture and authenticity to your story.

Who knows? A whole story could come out of a single artifact you see in the museum!

12

Archaeology

WHEN I SUGGEST THAT ARCHAEOLOGY IS SOMETHING that will help you to enrich your novel and help you do research, I'm not suggesting that you arm yourself with a leather jacket, fedora and whip - though that would be a lot of fun!

Archaeology can help us not only in touching the past (very carefully!), but more importantly in understanding the places and landscapes that belong to the period and setting of your novel. By looking at archaeological reports, documentaries (Who doesn't love the show Time Team?) and other sources, you can see the layout of buildings, and understand how a structure was used. If you are writing about imperial Rome, then archaeological reports might help you to understand the various structures on the Palatine Hill and what they were used for.

Landscapes are also important in archaeology. For one novel, I used archaeological reports to understand the evolution and uses of a landscape about a particular Iron Age hillfort where much the novel was set. These reports were extremely useful in bringing the setting to life, understanding the activities of the people living around the hillfort, and what was happening on the site itself.

If you live in the United Kingdom, or another country where it is permitted, you might also be able to volunteer on an archaeological dig to gain some experience (if that interests you), but also to get to know the landscape around a site much more intimately. By spending time there, digging and getting dirty, you will get to know how a place feels and smells, how the light falls and colours look at various times of day. It may sound silly, but all of this adds to the richness of your descriptions in your novel.

Archaeologists today are busy creating amazing resources for us, building 3D models of historical sites that can allow us to walk through historic sites and landscapes from the comfort of a couch across the sea. And with the advent of virtual reality, the prospect of actually stepping into the past is even more exciting.

Remember, archaeologists are not just into old things, they are on the cutting edge of technologies and methods that are bringing the past to life.

13

Living History

WHEN IT COMES TO LIVING HISTORY, MANY PEOPLE will imagine a lone student dressed up in period clothing, lurking in the corner of a heritage home waiting to be asked questions, or actors at a Renaissance fair dressed in pantaloons and speaking with a bad English accent. Both of these can be true to an extent when it comes to living history, but there is much more to it.

Living history demonstrations and historical re-enactors are a wonderful resource for authors of historical novels.

You can find living history re-enactors at many historical sites doing demonstrations throughout the summer season, so if you have a trip planned, or live near a historical site that dates to your chosen period, you should definitely go and check it out. Be sure to speak to the re-enactors, for they are often serious enthusiasts who do a lot of research and use their knowledge to teach others. They can inform historians and archaeologists about the practical aspects, production, and workings of various items found by archaeologists. For example, a serious re-enactor can tell you how comfortable it is to wear armour and how easy it is to fight in. That is good information. They might even let you try on their helmet!

As far as Medieval or Renaissance fairs, if you can look past the bad accents, dodgy meats and giant pickles, it can indeed be inspiring to walk through a sort of Medieval marketplace to get a vague sense of setting for your novel. It is noisy, smelly, colourful and full of life, and that may be exactly what you want for your novel. You can even purchase something to inspire you as you write, such as a new wool cloak, or a sword reproduction (if you are going to write battle scenes, you need to know what it is like to swing a sword to get a feel for what is possible!). The great thing about these products is that they are most often made by local or travelling artists and craftspeople who are enthusiasts of history just like you! Why not support them?

Heading to a fair can be a really fun part of your research. My favourite is the Michigan Renaissance Festival, but there are fairs all over the place during the summer, so check which ones are closest to you.

Tip: There are many Facebook groups for historical re-enactors of almost any historical period. Join these groups and ask your questions. They will be more than happy to answer.

14

Maps

When it comes to research for your historical novel, maps are crucial to understanding the world and setting you are writing about.

Knowing where roads were located, the distances, topography, place names, mines, ports etc. is crucial. Sometimes, there is information that is missing, so you can take some liberties, but otherwise, if you get the geography wrong, people will call you on it and you could lose readers.

Try to find maps that pertain to your period. One particularly useful range of maps are the Ordnance

Survey maps for the United Kingdom. These are highly detailed, and they even have a range of historical maps such as a map of Roman Britain, or historical city maps such as Viking York. If you can get a map such as this for your chosen time and place it will be invaluable to you in writing your novel.

There are also interactive maps online that can help you to calculate distances for various methods of travel in your world. One particularly useful one for the Roman period is ORBIS, Stanford University's geospatial network model of the Roman world.

Find the resources that apply to your story and use them.

15

Photos

MOST OF US LOVE LOOKING AT PHOTOS. THEY ALLOW us to see places from great distances, to study them. They fire our imaginations and inspire us. Photos are truly worth a thousand words, and today, with billions of photos available online, it is easier than ever to research historical sites, artifacts and landscapes. Just do an image search on Google and you will likely get hundreds or thousands of photos to look at. There are also online archives of photos (historical and modern) of archaeological sites that you can look at to get inspired and help you understand sites.

Aerial photographs and drone footage of historic sites and landscapes are also extremely useful to the historical novelist, and help archaeologists and historians to make new discoveries all the time. Be sure to search for these too. They will give you a bird's-eye view of your chosen historic site. If the discovery is recent, you could even be the first novelist to include a site in his or her work!

16

Toponymics

ONE AREA OF RESEARCH THAT YOU MAY NOT BE familiar with is toponymics. 'Topos' is the Greek for 'place'. Toponymics is the study of place names.

If your novel is set in a particular area, it would be worth stepping back and looking at the places names. They can tell you a lot about a region, what went on there, what a town was used for, and give you hints as to any events that might have taken place there.

Granted, this area of research is a bit more advanced, but it could give added depth to your novel.

Who knows? You could even uncover something yourself!

17

Numismatics

ONE AREA OF RESEARCH THAT MANY MIGHT FIND unexpected here is numismatics, or the study of coinage. Coins can be a brilliant resource for your as you gather information for your novel and period of history. Coins can tell you a lot about history for they were used not only as a way of obtaining goods, but also as propaganda, to commemorate important people or historical events.

And there are many coins from any given historical period, so you should be able to find them for yours either online, in books, or at your local museum.

There are a couple of examples of how coins have helped me in my own research in the past. Firstly, when I wanted to know what a particular imperial family looked like, I was able to view a Roman coin hoard at a local museum that was filled with silver coins of that particular family. They were in magnificent condition, so I was able to see details like the women's hair styles, the men's beards and even the nature of their personality from the way their faces were portrayed. The coins helped me to get to know that family even before I started writing!

A more recent example is when writing about a funeral for an emperor that the primary sources said involved one of the largest funeral pyres ever. But, I could not find any descriptions or later engravings of this funeral pyre. I did not know what it looked like. Then, I started looking online and came across a single photo of a rare coin that had been minted to commemorate the funeral of this emperor. On one side of the coin, was a detailed image of the funeral pyre itself!

Remember, coins are not just for buying things, they are snapshots of the past that can help you in your research. Learn the denominations of coins for your period of history, find out or approximate how much things might have cost at that time, and you will add depth to your story that few others have.

18

Religion

THIS IS PERHAPS ONE OF THE MOST IMPORTANT aspects of your historical novel.

Today, religion has a bit of a bad reputation, and some writers may be loathe to explore religious doctrines, ideals or practices in their novels.

However, if you don't include some aspect of religion in your historical novel, you will be doing your book, and your readers, a disservice.

Religion may not play as important a role in people's lives today, but it was central to people's lives throughout history. In some cases, such as the

Crusades, it was the impetus for many historical events.

If you really want to get to know your characters and historical period, to accurately portray history for your readers, you should think very seriously about including religion and religious practices in your book.

But how do you find information on religions and religious practices if you are not familiar with them?

When it comes to the 'revealed' religions such as Judaism, Christianity, or Islam for example, you should not have any trouble finding websites, books and more about them in intimate detail. You can even speak with a rabbi, minister, or imam if you have specific questions about beliefs and practices. And remember the academics, for they too will be able to help you understand these and other religions.

If the religion you are writing about is ancient, and the practices and exact beliefs are less-known or completely unknown, then there are other ways you can gather information. The carvings and reliefs on ancient altars, monuments and statuary can give you clues about practices such as what was usually offered to a particular god or goddess, the sort of language used, the types of sacrifices or offerings that were usually given, and what the priests or priestesses wore.

Archaeological remains such as temples can also give you clues about the religious practices of the past, and the types of ceremonies. For example, the ceremonies for Jupiter in the temple on the Capitoline hill in Rome would have differed greatly from ceremonies for Mithras held in the caves on the fringes of the Roman Empire.

If you cannot find all the information you need from books and academic papers, or from archaeological sites and monuments, then as an author, you are able to fill in the gaps and take some liberties with the unknown. Just make sure you note this in the Author's Note at the back of your book, especially if it plays a large role in the story.

Don't be afraid of religion as an author. Embrace it so that your characters and their world can come to life.

19

Myths, Legends, and Folklore

THIS SUBJECT TIES IN WITH RELIGION IN A WAY, FOR during some periods (e.g. Ancient Greece), myth, legend and folklore were a part of religious beliefs, as gods were more 'human' compared with other periods.

Myths, legends and folklore are a cultural lifeblood. The tales were not just bedtime stories told to children around a fiery hearth, but they were considered history, fact. Myths, legends and folklore are not only part of a people's belief system, they are central to the identity of a people. Even Alexander the

Great slept with a copy of the *Iliad* beneath his pillow at night!

Read the myths and legends or folkloric tales that pertain to the period of your novel and get a sense of the ideals and mores portrayed in them, the lessons that were being taught to readers or listeners. If you can, visit or study the sites associated with those myths, legends and heroes of folklore. It will help you to better understand the mindset of the people during your period of history.

Remember, every myth or legend has its base in fact, so who's to say they did not actually happen?

20

Travel

I'VE SAVED THIS CHAPTER FOR LAST IN THIS SECTION because travel can be tricky. Whether for financial reasons, safety reasons, or just the difficulty of physical transport to a particular location, it is not always possible to travel to the places about which you are writing.

However, if you can travel, it is perhaps the most important part of your research. Few things compare to standing in the place where your characters live and roam. You can feel things, smell things, hear things, and see things that your reading and online research cannot possibly give you.

I was once told by a novelist writing about the Crusades that he went to the Middle East to do research, and while there, he licked stones to see how the dirt and dust felt and tasted on his tongue so that when he wrote, it would be all the more realistic.

That doesn't mean to say you should go licking historic monuments, but it does mean that actually going to a historic place can make the difference between your novel and descriptions being good, or great.

If you can't possibly travel, try speaking with people who have actually been there. If you are writing about an ancient war in Afghanistan but don't feel safe travelling there, try speaking to a soldier who has done a tour there about what it was like. Ask them what the views were like, the vegetation, the smells etcetera. Get as much information from them as they are willing to give, then acknowledge their contribution at the end of the book, and send them a copy.

If you are writing about imperial Rome, however, then it might be easier to visit and walk the streets your characters will walk. If Robin Hood is your main character, take a walk through Sherwood Forest, smell the air and feel the bark of those ancient oak trees.

There are few substitutes for actually visiting a site, so if you can possibly manage it, travel can be one of the best, most informative forms of research for your novel.

Once you have gathered all the information you need through various forms of research, and immersed yourself in the world and time about which you are writing, then what?

You start writing.

PART II

WRITING

INTRODUCTION

In the previous section, you learned about the various ways in which you can do the research for your historical novel. Once you have done that, and are intimately acquainted with the world and people featured in your novel, it is time to start writing.

This can be a most daunting task for any writer. Typing those first few words, sentences and paragraphs can make you sweat as if you were a foot soldier staring down a charge of heavy cavalry.

Don't worry.

At this point, you are well-armed because you have done your research and know your history. You know the people and places you are going to write about, and like a general setting out for war, you know that though you have battles ahead of you, victory is within your grasp.

You just have to start, and keep on marching.

This section is not about the craft of writing. There are plenty of books on writing craft out there.

In this section on writing, you will learn various tips and tricks to help you get through your first draft and turn it into the epic that you have dreamed of.

21

A Well-Planned Campaign

Before you throw that first spear and really get stuck into your novel, there are some questions you can ask yourself that, if you have the answers, will make things much easier for you down the road.

Writing a novel is like a military campaign in a way, so if you can make some decisions before you set out, you will be much more efficient and able to concentrate on writing.

Assuming you know your genre well, and have read other successful authors in it (if not, go and read a few in your genre), there are some questions that you can ask yourself in order to determine your goals.

- Is this going to be a series of books or a standalone novel? There are differences between those options, and series will make an author more money, so you need to know which one you want to pursue, or leave the door open for a possible sequel.
- What is your objective? Are you trying to entertain, enlighten (e.g. reveal the hardship of slaves?), teach history in an interesting way, or explore new ideas or theories?
- Who is your target audience? There will be more on your 'ideal reader' in Part IV on Marketing, but it helps to know this. No novel is interesting to everyone.
- Are you going to outline your novel, or are you going to make things up as you go? This will relate to whether or not you decided to write a series or a standalone novel.

If you can answer these questions for yourself before you really get started on writing your novel, then you will thank yourself later. The general who plans his or her campaign ahead of time is much more likely to have fewer surprises and be victorious in the end.

Tip: To help you keep track of all the information you've gathered and separate your chapters, it is worth investing in writing software such as Scrivener or Vellum. These are excellent project management tools for writers, and they also create the e-book and paperback files you will use later to publish so that you don't have to pay someone else to do that for you.

22

The Power of Plotting

When I wrote my first two novels, I was a 'pantser', someone who made things up as they went. I thought it was more creative and fulfilling to do so. That is true to an extent, but it is also very slow and can lead to continuity problems later in the book or series that you have to go back and fix.

There is a misconception out there that if you plot out your novel, you will miss out on the surprises that occur when a story takes over and the Muse starts speaking through you.

This is not true.

After going from a 'pantser' to a 'plotter', I became a much more efficient and productive writer with stories that were cleaner and tighter. When I started plotting my novels, I didn't create long, multi-page descriptions of every single chapter. Rather, there were a few bullet points highlighting the main events or plot points that were to occur for each chapter. I had direction, but the writing was still full of surprises that were highly fulfilling on a creative level.

The truth is that the historical novelist has an advantage over writers in other genres because the history itself is a guideline for your plot. If your story is about a well-known figure of history, then you know what you have to write. If your main character is fictional, but exists in a world surrounded by historical people or events, you still know what you have to write. The job of the historical novelist is to fill in the gaps between what is known and to take readers into the minds of the characters.

Basically, if you even do a little plotting, you will be more organized, efficient, and ready to undertake your novel campaign.

. . .

Tip: Create a timeline of the historical events that will occur during your novel. It can be a simple line across a horizontal piece of paper with events and dates. Beneath this historical timeline, create another timeline for your characters so that you know where they are and what happens to them during the history of your story.

23

Character Sketches

JUST AS A PLOT FOR YOUR NOVEL WILL HELP YOU TO stay on track during your writing, so too will character sketches. As you get further into your story, you will be adding more and more characters. It will be difficult to keep track of them as you go.

Character sketches can be an important reference for you as they contain details about appearance (e.g. hair and eye colour, or weapon of choice), or personal background (e.g. Where are they from? What are their parents' or children's names?). There are a lot of details that go into creating a solid, three-dimensional character that your readers can truly connect with and feel for, so you want to remain consistent whenever you are referring to them.

Tip: Create a reference guide or 'bible' for your novel where you put all of your character descriptions, research materials, sketches, maps etc. This will be a living document throughout the creation of your novel or series. Add new characters as you go, as well as details about places, events and so on. Trust me, you will go back to this reference guide again and again.

24

Every Hero has a Journey

SOME OF YOU MAY ALREADY BE AWARE OF THE concept of 'the Hero's Journey' which was developed by Joseph Campbell. It is often mentioned in writers' circles, and with good reason.

The importance of the Hero's Journey, as Campbell outlined it, rings true at every turn and across cultures, and it can be one of your most important allies throughout the plotting and writing of your novel or series. If it was good enough to help George Lucas write Star Wars, it is certainly good enough for you.

The Hero's Journey can help you when you are plotting, but also when you get stuck during your writing. It is not a cliché. It is a guide and, some might say, the soul of storytelling around the world.

If you haven't read Joseph Campell's work, then you need to check it out. You can start with *The Hero with a Thousand Faces*. Alternatively, watch Bill Moyers' *The Power of Myth* interview with Joseph Campbell in which the latter speaks at length about his research, philosophy, and the Hero's Journey. You won't regret it.

Another, more complex story plotting method that uses Joseph Campbell's philosophy of the Hero's Journey is Sean Coin's *Story Grid* architecture. Coin, a friend and editor of historical novelist Steven Pressfield, has developed a more detailed hero's journey within a story architecture that is common to major publishing and Hollywood blockbusters. It is also worth checking out, as Coin knows what he is talking about.

Don't let these methods of plotting or story architecture daunt you. You can be flexible within these systems, and the uniqueness of your story and you as a writer will absolutely shine through.

Remember, the universality of the human experience across time and peoples is something you can tap into, an ally and guide throughout your own journey as a writer.

25

Storyboarding

STORYBOARDING IS SOMETHING THAT IS USED BY filmmakers all the time, but it can also be useful to authors of historical fiction and fantasy.

We're not talking about drawing pictures of every scene however, though that is what filmmakers do. What we are looking for here is a quick reference or visual aid to have beside you as you write. It will be very helpful. Indeed, the act of creating a storyboard can help you with plotting and give you a visible finish line or goal to aim for.

. . .

Tip: Take a sheet of paper. Turn it horizontally and draw three rows of four squares across, making a total of twelve squares on the page. Each square is a chapter in your book. In point form, within each chapter's square, write the order of events, main plot points, twists etc. that will occur.

This is not a super detailed outline, but rather a quick guide to keep you on track and see your story at a glance. You can also do this on a computer or with sticky notes. Add pages and squares as needed.

26

Sketching

At the outset of your writing campaign, or if you are stuck in the middle, sketching a setting or scene can help free the creativity and get you back on track.

Concept designs are used in film all the time, so why not use them for books?

In one of my novels, I wasn't quite sure how to play out a particular scene set in a settlement on a lake. A lot was going to happen, but I wasn't sure where the action should take place, or indeed what the place looked like in detail. The idea was still fuzzy.

So, I decided to sketch it out (and I am terrible at drawing), and doing that helped me to get a clear vision of the setting and scene, allowing me to continue writing.

Tip: Battle scenes can be complex and chaotic. If you have battle scenes in your historical novel, try sketching out the location. Add troop movements, stand-offs for main characters etc. Add numbers for the various actions in the order they take place, and then write in that order for good flow to your story.

27

Discipline was a Goddess

THE ROMAN ARMY WAS ONE OF THE MOST SUCCESSFUL fighting forces in the ancient world, and to the Romans, Discipline, or 'Disciplina', was a goddess. Every night on campaign, after marching twenty to twenty-five miles, they made a camp surrounded by a ditch and palisade. Early the next morning, they would get up, strike camp, fill in the ditches, and march the next twenty to twenty-five miles. This routine required discipline, and it led to many victories for Rome.

When it comes to writing, discipline and a routine are essential for success.

Professional authors will tell you there is no such thing as 'writer's block'. They will tell you that writing and finishing books requires them to sit down every day and write, no matter what.

Some people are more creative during the early morning, others late at night. Think about what your optimal creative time of day is, and try to write at that time.

Decide on a routine and stick to it with the discipline of the Roman army.

If you do this, the writing will get easier and easier as you go, the longer you are in the routine. If it doesn't work for you, try something new until you find what works.

I used to write during my lunch breaks at work, but this was the time of day when I was most tired or rushed. As a result I wrote less, and what I wrote required a lot more heavy editing. After a few years working like that, I was pushed to finish a long-expected novel, but I was finding it hard to get to the finish line. So, I changed my routine. I started getting up at five in the morning every day, even on weekends, and writing during my optimal creative time for a couple of hours before work, or before the house was astir. The result? I finished the book, and then another, and another, each one taking less time than the previous one. My production shot up because I found a routine that worked for me and I stuck to it.

Find what works for you and maintain your discipline. You will be victorious!

28

Decide on a Theme

ONE OF THE BEST PIECES OF ADVICE I HAVE READ when it comes to writing a novel came from author Steven Pressfield.

He advised that a writer should decide on a solid theme for a novel and then stick with that theme for the duration.

He was right.

It might not be easy to decide on a theme at first, but as you plot your novel or write it, it will emerge. When it does, you should stay on theme. Everything you write, every scene or character's action should be 'on theme'.

This advice first helped me with a novel about the ancient Olympic Games. I decided that the theme of the novel would be 'There can be no victory without sacrifice'. I wrote this theme down on a piece of paper and kept it within view when I was writing. I looked at everything I wrote through the lens of this theme. The result was that I wrote one of the most well-crafted, solid stories of my career to that point.

Before you start writing, think about the possible themes for your novel. Once you have one in mind, make it your mantra for the duration of your novel.

29

Get Your Story Down!

THE IMAGE OF A WRITER STARING AT A BLANK PAGE for hours or days is a common one, but as authors, it does us little good. There is much ado about writing the first words or pages of a novel, let alone the saggy middle, plot twists, an ending that hits the reader over the head, and all the other little nooks and crannies of a story. There is a lot to potentially worry about.

But you shouldn't worry.

Don't psyche yourself out.

Just start your novel.

By this point, you're ready.

Some days, you will write thousands of words, and other days you may write only fifty. That's all right. As long as you write something, you have forward motion.

One of the best pieces of writing advice I've ever received came from my mentor, the late poet Leila Pepper. She said not to worry about researching more, editing, or anything else while you are writing. The important thing is to just get the story down on paper (or the computer). Get it down, get it out of your head. Once that is done, you have a story, something to work with.

The big battle can come once you get there, but you have to march to that place first. Keep marching, keep writing. You may have small skirmishes or stresses along the way, but that's ok. You can handle those. Just get through the first draft.

Get your story out of your head. Just get your story down!

30

A Crappy First Draft is Good

ONE OF THE MOST CREATIVELY-DESTRUCTIVE AND disheartening things for a writer is the expectation of perfection right out of the gate, that the first draft is going to win you a golden laurel wreath, and that you will be lauded by the world.

This expectation is unrealistic, and can stop you even before you start writing.

Accept that your first draft will be crap and will require a lot of work, especially if it is a first book. This approach or perspective will free you!

If you can make this mental shift, you will just write and worry about it later. Before you know it, you'll have a completed novel to work with. Allow yourself to write poorly with the first draft.

Again… Just get the story down!

31

The Perils of Writers' Groups

YOU MIGHT BE TEMPTED TO SHARE BITS OF YOUR WIP (work in progress) in a writers' group. After all, writing is a solitary endeavour, and a little shop talk with a glass of chianti or chardonnay might seem like just the ticket.

Don't do it.

By all means, get together with other creatives and drink, have fun, talk, but don't share parts of your WIP. In fact, don't even describe the plot to them.

One bit of criticism can freeze you in the middle of writing your novel.

If you want to share your WIP, wait until the first draft of your novel is finished. If you need craft advice from a writers' group, do so by sharing short stories or speaking generally about a method, but never about your current project.

You might say that your group is highly positive and that the members don't tear each other down. That may be (and that's great!), but writers are no less prone to egotism than anyone else. A put-down in the middle of writing is not worth it. Not everyone sees eye-to-eye with you. You know your story better than anyone else. A bit of criticism during your first draft, even if well-intentioned, could throw you off balance and make you doubt your plot or writing choices.

32

Get out into the World

WRITING CAN BE EXTREMELY ISOLATING AND solitary. Let's face it, as writers, we love to get lost in the worlds we create. We can go for days without speaking to a person outside of our story.

However, when you are in the middle of writing, burnout remains a definite possibility. Solitude can be helpful, but loneliness can be damaging. This is partially a mindset thing, but it can affect you and your writing just when things are going well.

The Romans worked hard, but even they had furloughs now and again.

As part of your disciplined routine, allow for time with family and friends, exercise, cultural activities, or anything else that you enjoy. If you do this, then you can refill your creative well and be fresh for your next writing session.

Tip: Throw a dinner party for friends in which you make dishes from the historical period of your book. It's fun, inspiring, and you are still in the world of your novel, sharing a part of that world. Food can be a wonderful conversation piece!

33

Reaching 'The End'

EVERY WRITER DREAMS OF THIS PART.

You've been harried by enemies along the march, by dreaded self-doubt. You've fought many battles along the way. It's been tough, no doubt, a journey of agony and ecstasy.

However, your training, knowledge, and discipline have got you through to the final battle, and you've come out victorious.

You've typed 'The End'.

A lot of people react differently to this. Some will scream, or do a dance. Others will weep. Some might even be in denial and find an excuse to keep tweaking things, even though the story is written. We are all different, and we deal with reaching the end of our journeys in different ways.

We all come back to our own private Ithacas changed.

When you type 'The End', be sure to pause and enjoy it. It will feel amazing. After all, many people say they want to, or should, write a book, but few have actually done it!

You have, and you should enjoy the weight of those laurels upon your brow.

You are now a part of the creative elite. You have moved up the ranks.

Yes, there is more work to be done, but you really should be proud and pause to savour the moment.

You deserve it!

Tip: Reward yourself when you finish the first draft of a novel. Celebrate finishing by doing something you enjoy. You might want to go out to dinner, or get a bottle of your favourite wine to savour. Whatever works for you, do it when you type those precious, sought after words 'The End'.

34

Set Your Book Aside

ONCE YOU HAVE FINISHED THE FIRST DRAFT OF YOUR historical fiction or historical fantasy novel, you will be tempted to read it right away.

Don't.

Avoid the temptation to read your newly-finished novel. You are too close to it. It will be your 'Precious', and we all know how that plays out!

When you have a completed first draft, make sure to set the manuscript aside for at least a month. Truthfully, the longer you can set it aside (without practicing avoidance!), the better. You need time apart, some distance.

If you can set your novel manuscript aside, and work on other projects, you can come back to it when you are fresh, rejuvenated, and less attached to every word. You won't mind making the tough decisions that editing requires, and you will be reading it as more of an 'outsider'.

Trust me on this. When you have finished your first draft, set it aside and let it simmer for a while. You need a clear head when you finally do get down to the first reading.

35

The First Reading

THE FIRST READING OF YOUR HISTORICAL NOVEL IS only for you.

This is important.

After your month or more of having set it aside and kept your distance, print it and read it.

Printing allows you a different perspective than reading it on a screen, which is likely where you wrote it in the first place. It will also prevent you from doing accidental 'quick edits' as you go, or deleting parts that you may miss later.

As you read, mark things as you go such as typos,

information gaps or factual errors or question marks, continuity issues, things to possibly cut etc. It helps to create an editing legend with different colours for each of the categories just mentioned.

Don't be afraid of this process. Enjoy it! Because you let your manuscript sit for a while, oftentimes the parts you thought were garbage will surprise you by how good they are. If there are parts of your novel that were garbage (and there should be, because you've allowed yourself to write a crap first draft!), you can easily clean them up because no one else will have read the novel but you.

Enjoy the first reading of your novel. It is your chance to watch your creation come to life.

Tip: The first draft is only for you. Don't let anyone else read it until you have made your edits and have a second draft ready to go. If you are writing a series, keep a list of things that need to happen in the next book, things to carry forward in the story arc of your series.

If you are writing a book that uses words from another language (e.g. Latin or ancient Greek), keep a list of these non-English words so that you can create a glossary at the end of the book.

You should also keep track of the historical events in your novel so that you can address them in your Author's Note at the end. An author should always highlight what is historically accurate, and where some artistic license was taken with the history. Your readers, who are history-lovers, will appreciate this.

36

Don't Throw Anything Away

As you edit your historical novel, you may find a lot of extraneous detail, unneeded passages, overly long descriptions or back story. History buffs do love to share the information we have researched by giving the occasional information dump in the middle of a novel. If you have any of these extras littered throughout your novel, you will need to cut them.

But don't throw them away completely! Save them in a separate folder.

Why? They might be useful later on.

Here's an example. When I wrote my first novel, I

included a whole lot of back story for my main protagonist. I was eager to develop his character and to allow readers to get to know him intimately. However, it was too much information. So, I had to cut enormous passages from the novel.

The things I cut were good, but they just didn't belong where I had initially placed them.

A few years later, I wanted to create a prequel novel as a sort of lead magnet (more on that in Part IV on Marketing), so I took this deleted back story information about my protagonist and based a full-length novel around it.

That novel became an immediate #1 Bestseller on Amazon (for several months!) in its categories and helped me to more than double the salary of my full-time day job!

Trust me on this. Don't throw anything away. You never know what it may turn into.

37

The Second Draft

WHEN IT COMES TO THE SECOND DRAFT OF YOUR historical novel, be sure to stick with your previous routine. Maintain the discipline that got you through your first draft so that you can make the necessary edits to complete your second draft.

If you've written long-hand, as some authors do, your second draft can be what you type out. Be warned, however, that doing it this way can be slower and can leave typos as your fingers go to work on the keys. If you have typed in the first place, corrections will be easy to make.

Remember to keep that folder of deleted materials as you go.

38

Don't Over Edit

Many writers are prone to overthinking things, especially if they are seeking perfection. This can turn the editing process into a never-ending loop that you cannot extract yourself from, like Theseus without a thread to lead him out of the labyrinth.

Some years ago, in a masterclass with historical novelist Bernard Cornwell, our group received an excellent piece of advice from this acclaimed historical fiction writer.

'Don't over edit!'

And he was right. No book is perfect, and yours is

no exception. We are our harshest judges when it comes to our writing, and if we expect perfection, we will never stop editing.

At one point, you have to stop editing and give your second draft to others to read.

Listen to Bernard Cornwell and don't over edit!

39

Beta Readers

ONCE YOU ARE HAPPY WITH YOUR EDITED HISTORICAL novel (whether you did a second, third or fourth draft) you will need to hand it off to another set of fresh eyes.

Every general needs to call on reinforcements at some point.

Our brains fill in gaps, and errors do tend to slip by, even if you are the most astute person and use fancy grammar software.

If you can afford editors, do use them, but if not,

beta readers are your best option. Here are some things to look for in a beta reader:

- They should be someone who likes history and historical fiction/fantasy
- They should be someone who likes and is familiar with the period of history your novel is set during
- Ideally, they should understand what you are trying to do (think back to your goals in writing your novel)
- They should be someone who matches the profile of your ideal reader or target audience

You should not have so many beta readers that you cannot manage all of the input they may have, and communication they may require, but you should also have enough so that even with those who don't get back to you (yes, that does happen), you will still have enough useful input.

Tell your beta readers what to look for if you have

specific worries. Give them some guidance so that you can get the most out of their input. You don't have to listen to everything they say, but if something is brought up by two or more beta readers, you should have a close look at what they are saying and consider the change.

Be sure to remember these people in the Acknowledgements section at the end of your book.

40

You Have a Book! Now What?

It has been a very long road to this point. You've gone from idea to completed first draft, through several edits until, at last, you have a fully completed, polished historical novel.

It's the end of your campaign. You have victory!

Now what?

It's time to get your novel out into the world.

There will be temptations to fine-tune, to change things, tweak things you see as imperfect, but you should avoid these temptations. Don't over edit, especially if your beta readers are happy and you've taken their input into consideration and made some of those changes.

IT (Information Technology) people have an expression they use which is 'minimum viable product'. This is an interesting concept, and it can be helpful when putting a piece of work out into the world. It may be counter-intuitive to us as creatives, as authors, but because no book is perfect, it can be helpful. IT people will release a product and then provide bug fixes and updates as issues emerge. The main thing is to get the product out.

The good thing about your books is that, because you've edited and had beta readers, you likely have much more than a minimum viable product.

So, you need to get your book out into the world for people to read.

But how? How do you do this?

In the next section, we will look at some publishing options for your work of historical fiction and historical fantasy.

PART III

PUBLISHING

INTRODUCTION

Once you have a finished manuscript for your historical novel, it's time to publish. For you to do this, there are some options for you to be aware of, and decisions to make.

In this section, you will learn about the publishing options available to you so that you can make an informed decision that is right for you, your book, and your career as an author of historical fiction or historical fantasy.

Let's get to it!

41

The World of Publishing

In the past decade (it is now late 2019), the publishing industry has experienced massive changes. These changes have upset the old guard, and industry 'gatekeepers' as they are called, but the truth is that it really is the best, most opportune time in history to be a writer.

It has never been easier for a writer to reach an audience and to have direct contact with the readers who could sustain their career. The online world is vast, and if you can find the people who will champion your work, good things will happen.

The downside is that there is a lot of noise and competition for people's attention online too. As an author, you and your work have to stand out and be made available in more than just one store. The little bookshop down the street will no longer keep an author's career afloat by stocking their book and inviting them to speak and sign books.

You need to decide what you want out of publishing.

- Do you want a full-time career as an author?
- Do you just want to *say* you are 'published' and are not concerned with money?
- How hard are you willing to work?
- How much is your book worth to you? (this goes beyond money)
- Where do you want to see your book sold?
- What are your long-term and short-term goals as an author?

These questions and more are important to ask yourself so that you don't head down the wrong path on this part of the journey and waste precious time.

That is why you need to understand the options before you. To begin with, we'll look at the two main publishing routes open to you in this new world: Traditional Publishing, and Independent Publishing.

In the next few chapters, we will look at both of these.

42

Traditional Publishing

Historical fiction has long been in the domain of traditional publishing. It is an old industry with global reach (especially when it comes to paperbacks and hard covers), and traditional publishers have the relationships with the big bookstore chains.

For a long time, authors and creatives have held to the dreamy idea of the successful writer who gets a publishing deal, makes a lot of money, and is swept around the country to do book signings and speak with adoring fans. The thought of your only job being to write, while taking hefty advances for each book, going on tours, drinking champagne at award ceremonies etcetera is highly appealing. Who wouldn't like that?

Traditional publishers have tremendous marketing power and the money to back it. If they decide to really back you as an author, then who knows? Perhaps that book tour will happen for you!

But…

Times have changed in the publishing industry, and the old ideas held to for so long by the traditional publishing world are being challenged. In a fast-changing online world, the big traditional publishers are having to find new ways of doing things to survive, especially if they want to weather the storm and compete with the major online retailers who are sweeping across the world like the Huns across Europe.

There are pros and cons to going the traditional publishing route, and you need to take a serious look at them before you take the plunge. You need to set romantic notions aside for the time being.

Traditional Publishing Pros

- Massive marketing power

- Big budgets
- A lot of cachet for you as an author
- Leader for hardcover and paperback distribution
- Relationships with big bookstore chains, public libraries, schools etc.
- Foreign language translation
- Audio book creation
- Potential advances or bonuses (the latter for well-known authors)
- Editors and artists on staff
- Respect in the industry

Traditional Publishing Cons

- Unwillingness to change old ideas and pivot in the face of change
- Gatekeepers (you have to be let into this world - *they* decide if your book is good enough)
- Little to no creative control for the author. Once you sign with them, the book is theirs
- Authors need to earn back their advances.

Few people realize that advances need to be earned back by the author's sales. It is not free money (that is a 'bonus'). The amount of an advance comes out of the initial profits
- They keep your rights for the duration of the contract
- Restrictive contracts
- If an author's book doesn't perform (as far as sales) in the first little while, they are quickly set aside
- Authors who don't have massive sales for their books are often relegated to the traditional publisher's mid-list where they can languish for years without any marketing support
- Low royalties. Authors typically receive twelve to fifteen percent royalty rates. This makes it difficult to have a full-time career unless you sell millions of copies

This is a lot to take in, and you will either maintain the romantic notion that has been every aspiring author's dream, or your bubble will burst. It need not be one or the other, because being informed is the key to making the decisions you need to make.

So, if you want to get into the world of traditional publishing and shoot for those stars so many have dreamed of, there is basically one way to do this: get a literary agent.

Literary agents are the middle men and women with whom the big publishers have relationships. They trust each other. Authors rarely get accepted by a big publisher through direct contact. It is done through a literary agent who decides to take you on and champion your work, for a commission of course.

Your first step is to query literary agents, but before you do this, you need to do some research. A historical novelist who writes about Iron Age Britain should not be querying an agent who represents authors who write contemporary romance novels, for example.

Try to find out if your favourite authors in your genre have agents and who they are (better yet, try to speak with them and get an introduction to their agent!). Look at agent websites and see who they represent and in what genres. Have they had successes for their authors? Do they have good or bad reviews online on sites like *Preditors and Editors* and *Writer Beware*?

Do your research when it comes to querying agents so that you can find one who is the right fit for you and your genre, and so that you don't waste time doing so. You have a career to get going! It can be difficult to find a literary agent who will get you a deal with a traditional publisher, but if you can find a strong ally for you and your work, you just might be one of the few who lives the dream.

Tip: Research literary agents and their contact information, and get more information on traditional publishing. Check such books as *Writer's Market* and the *Guide to Literary Agents* by Writer's Digest. You can also subscribe to industry newsletters such as *Publishers Marketplace* and *Publishers Weekly* to keep an eye on what agents are striking good deals for their authors.

43

Independent Publishing

THE REAL CHANGE IN THE PUBLISHING INDUSTRY IN the last decade has come about because of the rise of independent, or 'indie', publishing. The word 'change', is something of an understatement. It is a new world.

The old and, frankly, negative connotation of self-publishing, or 'vanity publishing', has disappeared as much as Carthage after Rome salted the earth of that fallen city. 'Self-publishing' is something of a misnomer anyway, as is 'independent' publishing. In the rapid changes that have occurred in the last ten years, indie authors and publishers have taken the 'self' out of the equation, and are hiring professional cover designers, editors, voice actors and more to put out products that rival those of any big, traditional publishing company. A whole new publishing industry has come to life online with many creatives in this new industry making full-time livings.

With the gatekeepers and middle men and women taken out of the equation, and the quality of independently-published books at a highly professional level, the previous negative aura is fast dissipating.

Many indie authors are earning up to five figures a month and quitting their day jobs to do what they love. And there have been many indies who have started earning six and seven figure incomes per year!

It really is an exciting time to be an author! Without needing an agent, or a traditional publisher to 'pick you', you can distribute your own work worldwide in both e-book and print (with the advent of print-on-demand technology, there is no overhead for print runs!).

So, with all of this excitement, and all of these options, where does an author with a ready manuscript publish?

The biggest player in the industry is, of course, Amazon. The company really kickstarted the indie publishing movement with their Kindle reading device, and by allowing authors to publish directly. But times are changing and competition to Amazon is emerging. Some of the places an author can publish directly, on a worldwide scale, are on Amazon KDP (Kindle Direct Publishing) and KDP Print, Apple Books, Google Play, Kobo and others.

If dealing directly with all of these companies is not for you, there are also well-respected aggregators who will distribute your e-books to all of them for you for a very small commission. A couple of these companies are Publish Drive and Draft2Digital, though there are many more out there.

The great thing about independent publishing and e-books is that as an author, you can receive a royalty rate of up to seventy-five percent (versus the twelve to fifteen percent of traditional publishing). The rate on paperbacks and hardcovers is lower because of costs of printing, but it still yields a good royalty. That is a huge difference. Here are some pros and cons to independent publishing:

Independent Publishing Pros

- Much higher royalties requiring fewer sales to make more money
- Full creative control over every aspect of your book
- You keep all your rights and copyrights
- Changes are easy as is the ability to pivot to meet fluctuations in the industry at any time
- Corrections can be made and uploaded in a matter of minutes
- An extremely helpful community of like-minded, creative people
- Myriad resources available to authors and publishers
- Worldwide distribution for e-books
- Hard work brings results
- Direct contact with readers
- No middle men/women, or gatekeepers deciding if you are good enough
- Extremely low cost of publishing (costs include cover design and editing, and later, advertising)
- A vast support industry of people who offer services

Independent Publishing Cons

- It can be overwhelming to do it all yourself
- Potential for burnout
- It is hard work (though the hard work does bear fruit!)
- Learning curve if you are starting from scratch and are unfamiliar with some of the technology
- No overnight successes. It is a long term game
- Sole responsibility for all marketing
- Potentially high costs of creating audio books and foreign language translations
- Lack of understanding or respect ('self-publishing' is still viewed by some people as a negative thing or cop-out)

When deciding between the traditional or independent publishing routes, there is a lot to consider. In some cases, successful indie authors have gone on to be offered big deals with traditional publishers. They have even signed movie deals with Hollywood! On the flip side, authors who were traditionally published and relegated to the midlist of big publishers have bought their rights back and breathed new life into their careers by independently publishing.

You need to think about what you want for your books and your career as an author of historical novels. Decide on a route, and do it right.

44

Know Your Rights

In your campaign to get your book out into the world, especially if you decide to go the traditional route of publishing, you need to know and protect your rights as an author. At the end of the day, big publishers are businesses, and they will do what benefits them the most.

There have been stories about authors being asked to sign contracts that grant the publisher 'world English rights'. This sort of blanket term potentially grants the publisher all e-book, paperback, hardcover, audio, film rights and more.

Never agree to anything like that.

Rights should be divided by territory (example: North American English vs. European English) and by format (an author might try to keep e-book rights and grant the publisher paperback rights). Remember, it's ok to negotiate when it comes to your contract, whether you do it yourself or through your agent who, hopefully, has your best interests at heart and can advise you.

When you are offered a publishing deal there can be a lot of excitement, a feeling of gratitude that someone has picked you and your book, or that you have finally 'made it'. It is exciting, to be sure, but don't be rash or make uninformed decisions because you'll regret it later on.

Be clear with your agent about what you want and what your long-term goals are. Ask questions so that you know your rights. Tell your agent what rights you want to keep.

I am not a lawyer, and none of this is legal advice, but I do highly recommend that if you are presented with a publishing contract you take it to an entertainment lawyer to review before you sign anything.

Remember to think long-term, and know your rights before signing.

. . .

Tip: Be sure to read the few books out there on legal questions or advice that are specifically geared toward authors. They have information on division of rights, contract negotiation etc.

45

Think Globally

IF YOU GO THE INDEPENDENT ROUTE, YOU WILL HEAR a lot about how many authors are making many thousands (even millions) of dollars on Amazon selling e-books.

In the early days, this was certainly true, but the 'kindle gold rush', as it was called, is over. You can still make quite a lot of money, but there is a lot more competition. Despite this, many authors still publish their work exclusively with Amazon KDP in a program called KDP Select. They do this in exchange for certain benefits such as 'Free Days' and being part of a pool to be paid for 'pages read'. We won't go into the details of KDP Select here. Just know that some authors are making a lot of money there.

But there is a problem.

It is generally agreed now that if an author wants to create a long-term publishing career for themselves, it is dangerous to put all of their eggs in one basket. Any company can change its terms and conditions at any time, and if an author is fully dependent on one company, that author's income could be wiped out overnight.

A company could decide that an author's work is in violation with their terms and conditions and decide to take down all of their books, thus eliminating their sales platform. In 2018, due to algorithmic changes in how books are presented in the online store, many author incomes on Amazon were cut in half.

This is serious.

If your author income disappears, what do you do?

That is why you should think globally, and think 'wide', as they say, by publishing on other platforms and nurturing readers in those places and other countries. You may not make as much money in those other stores at first but, given time, you will see those royalties creep up as you gain a broader reach for your books.

Other sellers and distributors will get your books out into the world. As mentioned earlier in this section, authors can publish directly through Apple Books, Kobo, Google Play and others, and the aggregator companies like Publish Drive and Draft2Digital will get your books into the non-English markets such as Italy, China, Germany and so many more.

You want to make it easy for anybody, anywhere, to find, buy and read your books. Think of the many millions of people around the world who have an iPhone or Android phone who could easily buy your book from Apple Books or from the Google Play store with the tap of an icon. It is pretty powerful, and if you do not have your books available in such places, you could be leaving a lot of money on the table by alienating thousands (or millions!) of potential readers.

When it comes to print books, there are also other options besides KDP Print. You can publish and distribute your books through companies such as Ingram Spark which have traditional paperback and hardcover print-on-demand options. These companies can be your gateway into traditional places like chain bookstores, schools, and public libraries. Print-on-demand is much more cost-effective for all parties, with the added bonus that it is much better for the environment.

The more streams of income you have for you as an author, the better. That way, if something goes awry in one of the stores, you still have the others to fall back on and keep the money coming in.

Think long-term, and think globally, for the world is much bigger than Amazon and the US market.

46

The Importance of Audio

For an author of historical fiction or historical fantasy, audio might seem like something of an extra, an extravagance. We like dusty old books, right? But at the time of writing this, audio is exploding!

The truth is that people are busy all the time, and more and more readers are consuming books through audio while they are doing other things. And with the advent of home assistants like Amazon's Echo, Apple's Siri, or Google Home, audio is becoming searchable.

In the past, Amazon's ACX and Audible were the only ways independent authors could create and sell audio books. However, that has changed with the advent of other companies who offer better royalties and broader distribution. Companies like Kobo and Findaway Voices are stepping up to compete with Amazon. Check out all of your options and make an informed decision.

One of the issues at the moment is the high cost of creating audio books, but this looks likely to improve with advances in the realm of AI (Artificial Intelligence). Services like Amazon Polly have the ability to take your book files and read them aloud (in a voice of your choosing) so that your work can be turned from text into speech. The technology is not perfect, but it is improving all the time.

Another way to cut the cost of creating an audio book, if you don't want to pay up front, is to do a 'royalty share' with an audiobook narrator/creator. If you go this route, just be aware that a large portion of the royalties will go to that other party for a set period of time.

If you are really trying to cut costs and want to create audio books, you can always narrate your own book. However, this is more difficult than it sounds for there is a certain way to do this, and audio book narrators often have voice training so that they can sustain reading over a long period of time. That said, a few authors have found a lot of success narrating their own audio books. If you can afford the equipment to create a decent recording, then this may be the option for you.

Whatever your plans are for publishing, audio books need to be a part of those plans. Otherwise, you'll still be using bronze in the Iron Age.

Tip: Author Joanna Penn has a lot of information about audio books and voice, and AI on her website and podcast, The Creative Penn.

47

Book Covers

THE OLD EXPRESSION THAT YOU SHOULDN'T JUDGE A book by its cover may be a nice sentiment, especially when the metaphor is applied to people (or writers!), but the truth is that people do. Potential buyers and readers of your book do judge it by the cover.

That is why your book cover, aside from good writing and a great blurb, is perhaps the most important item in your arsenal.

A good book cover stands out, even in the smaller scale of the online stores. It tells the reader in a few seconds what they can expect from your book, most importantly the genre (historical fiction or historical fantasy) and the period of history in which it is set (e.g. Imperial Rome, Medieval France, or Tudor England).

It can't be overstated enough how important the cover is in today's market. It could be argued that this is even more important than professional editing. If you are on a tight budget, the place to put your money is on the cover. If good research is your shield, and editing your armour, then the book cover is your sword. You can't win battles (or sell books) without a good one.

If you go the traditional route for publishing, you likely will not have any say in the sort of cover the publishing company puts on your book for various markets. It is their decision. However, if you are publishing independently, you get to decide because you have creative control.

Whether you do it yourself or hire a cover designer, you need to do research. Go online and check the top-selling books in your genre and categories. Get an idea of what sorts of covers sell. What works for other covers? Are there common traits among the top twenty?

By doing this, you can start to develop a picture of what your book cover could look like. If you are planning a series of books, keep this in mind so that you have a common look and feel to all of them.

If you have graphic design experience, then you will have an advantage when it comes to cover design because you can save a lot of money by doing it yourself. However, if you are not quite sure how to do it, don't chance it. Hire someone. This is too important an element. There are many cover designers online, most of whom will use stock images. Some authors who have the budget will commission original artwork for their books, which is fantastic, but this can be very expensive. You may need to start with stock images, and that is all right. Remember, as an independent author, you can change your covers at any time. Once you find a good cover designer who understands your genre, and with whom you have a good working relationship, hang onto them. They are one of your allies. Also make sure to acknowledge them at the end of your book.

When it comes to book covers, you cannot expect a cover designer to put every setting, every character, and basically tell the plot of your book on the cover. It would be too muddled. Keep it simple and eye-catching, clear about the genre and period of history. If your historical novel has more fantasy elements, you should make sure there is some fantasy element to the cover so as not to mislead potential readers.

One last thing to remember is that e-book, print, and audio book covers are all different sizes and are priced separately, so you need to be specific about what you need when you send a cover brief to your prospective designer.

At the end of the day, like a good sword, it is important to be proud of your book cover when you hold it and look at it, to be confident that it won't let you down when it counts.

Tip: Use programs like Canva to do a mock up of your cover idea with images. That way, you can be better prepared when approaching your cover designer. Remember, your cover has to pull readers in!

48

ISBNs

THE INTERNATIONAL STANDARD BOOK NUMBER, OR 'ISBN', is a ten or thirteen (after 2007) digit number that is unique to your book everywhere around the world. Even if someone does not have the title or author name for a book, this number is the key to tracking it down.

In the past, all books had ISBN numbers, but in the new publishing era, this is not always the case. For e-books published in stores like Amazon, authors have the option of not including an ISBN number because Amazon (for example) will assign its own number, an ASIN.

Independent authors and publishers don't have to have ISBN numbers for their books.

But it is a good idea.

If you want to 'go wide' and sell in many stores globally, and if you want to grow your business and career as an author, you should have your own ISBNs. Without an ISBN, you cannot get your books into stores, public libraries, schools, distribution catalogues etc. If you want all of that, it is essential. If you are independent, having an ISBN also registers your book to you and/or your publishing company.

If you are traditionally published, then you don't have to worry about this because the publisher will take care of it for you.

However, if you are independent you will need to make a decision about ISBNs because in many countries such as the US, authors have to pay to get ISBNs from companies such as Bowker. If you live in a country like Canada, you can get all the ISBNs you need for free from Library and Archives Canada. Find out how you can get ISBNs in your own country and then decide/budget accordingly for the future of your books and your career as a historical novel writer.

Remember too that every version of your book requires a separate ISBN. So, for example, if you have an e-book, paperback, hardcover and audio book version of your books, you will need four separate ISBNs.

For more information about ISBNs, check out the website for the International ISBN Agency.

49

A Storytelling Arsenal

AS A WRITER, IT IS IMPORTANT TO WRITE AND KEEP writing. In today's publishing world, it is also important to keep publishing so that you are not drowned out and forgotten in the chaos that is the online world.

But full-length historical novels are generally longer that most other genres of fiction. In a survey of its readers, Eagles and Dragons Publishing discovered that most readers prefer longer historical novels and that they were willing to wait for them in their favourite series.

However, you need to give your readers something in between novels. You also need to give yourself, as an author, a bit of a break, a palate-cleanser if you will, between your hefty historical tomes.

If you have just reached the end of your major work of historical fiction or historical fantasy, and need a break (as you most certainly will!), then you may want to try writing short stories or novellas. Doing this will help you to keep your skills honed as a writer, and you can try out new ideas that you can, perhaps, later expound on in a longer format.

These formats, in addition to your full-length feature novels, can be an important and strategic part of your storytelling arsenal.

Novellas are short novels. The exact length of a novella is not chiselled in stone and set up along the Appian Way, but generally, they can be anywhere from 20,000 to 60,000 words in length. Novellas are a great way to test out new ideas, but you can also use them to write a shorter side series. Who knows? They might even get you a whole new group of fans. Once you have a few novellas in a shorter series, you can also put those together in the form of a digital box set or omnibus paperback edition.

Novellas allow you to step outside of your creative comfort zone into new territory.

Short stories are, well, shorter than novellas and

can be anywhere from 300 to 20,000 words in length. These too can be good practice for a writer, and a sort of testing ground for new ideas. They can also be used as a free giveaway for readers and patrons between books, a way to keep people reading your words.

Don't underestimate short stories. They are more difficult to write than you think because you have to create a complete, cohesive story in a much shorter space. However, if you can master them, they will serve you well. Some authors make a full-time living from patrons, simply by writing weekly short stories!

Basically, if you combine using full-length novels, novellas, and short stories, you can have a lot of fun creatively, stay sharp as a writer, and create more possibilities for reaching an audience and keeping that audience.

Tip: If you have a box set for your series of books, add a novella related to that series as a bonus just for that box set.

50

Categorizing Your Book

ONE OF THE MOST IMPORTANT PARTS OF PUBLISHING, especially if you are an independent author/publisher, is choosing the correct categories for your books. This will help people to find your book when they are looking in the stores online, or browsing catalogues for stores, libraries and schools. It will also help search engines to pull up your books when people are searching online.

Before you choose categories for your book, do some research. Check books that are similar to yours and see what categories they are listed in. Are they bestsellers in those categories? Are there hidden categories that some books show up in? Is a particular category not too crowded? If not, then there is a chance for you to conquer some of that real estate!

When looking into what categories your book should be listed under, you will need to consider the categories in such online stores as Amazon (which has many non-traditional categories) as well as the BISAC (Book Industry Subject and Category) headings which are favoured by traditional stores, schools and libraries.

If your book is fiction, then you need to pick fiction categories, even if it is loaded with historical fact. This rule can be broken occasionally, depending on the store or distributor, but generally you should not mix fiction and non-fiction as it can confuse potential readers and lead to disappointment or even bad reviews.

If you can find categories that are open and underpopulated, you have more of a chance of hitting #1, so do your research carefully. Ask yourself which categories you would check to find books.

Categories also help the algorithms of online stores and search engines to find your books, and algorithms can be your allies if you know how to work with them.

51

Pricing

THIS IS AN AREA THAT HAS BEEN CONTROVERSIAL IN the past and will remain so. Big publishers want to make as much profit as possible, and independent author/publishers are struggling with valuing their work versus the best way to garner readers and make a profit.

When it comes to paperbacks, there are production and distribution or shipping costs, so you know roughly how much you need to charge for a book to make that money back and allow for a profit.

However, when it comes to e-books, there is no overhead. You don't need to charge a lot to make a profit.

The traditional publishing industry is grappling with this at the moment as it still charges high prices for e-books. Public libraries in particular have been vocal about the overcharging of big publishers when it comes to e-books.

Independent publishers however, have gone the other way and have been charging over fifty percent less than traditional publishers for e-books. And it has worked!

Despite lower prices, many independent publishers have been making more money from inexpensive e-books than the big publishers have done with paper. This is because of the lower costs and higher royalties available to independent authors and publishers.

In the days of the 'Kindle Gold Rush', some independent authors made millions of dollars by selling 0.99 cent e-books!

This may no longer be the case, but keeping your e-book prices low still works.

One strategy is to make the first book in your series available either for free or for sale for 0.99 or

1.99. This is a 'lead magnet' or 'funnel' that will draw readers into your series. The low price makes it easy for them to risk buying. From there, the price of subsequent books in a series can go up, but not too much. Generally, you will want to keep the price of your fiction e-books below 9.99, even though traditional publishers often charge over twelve dollars for an e-book.

One example is when Eagles and Dragons Publishing put out a full-length prequel novel to its main series. This was free for a couple of months, and then the price was raised to 0.99. The book had thousands of downloads and sales and made over seven thousand dollars for a few months. An added bonus, and the reason that series are such good money-makers, was that readers of that prequel novel went on to buy the subsequent books in the series!

A rising tide floats all boats, as they say.

With pricing, you want to think as a buyer and reader in your genre. What is attractive once the cover and blurb have grabbed their attention? The price.

It may be counterintuitive, but it works to price e-books lower.

Remember also to price by country, for books in other countries may be more or less expensive. You should also schedule sales and special price promotions to give your book or series an occasional boost.

When it comes to pricing, experiment until you find what works for you and your books, and what drives sales and profits.

52

Selling Direct

Even if you are selling and distributing your books around the world in several stores, you are most likely still relying on others to make that happen.

You need to sell in those stores, of course. After all, people are creatures of habit and like to go with what is familiar. They buy from stores they know. If they have a Kindle or iPhone, they will feel more comfortable buying books to read on Amazon or from Apple Books. It makes sense.

However, if the worst should happen and all those

other online book stores shut down, or block you for some reason, you need a safety net so that you don't lose all your income or readers. If you cannot sell your books from other stores all of a sudden (and this has happened to authors), how do you help readers and followers to continue to buy your work?

You sell to them directly.

At the end of the day, this is the ideal way to sell books because you know who is buying your books (retailers don't give you the names of those who buy your books), and you keep up to ninety-five percent of the profits.

To sell direct from your own website, you can use services like Selz, Payhip, or others to deliver your digital products for you for a small monthly fee. That way, your readers will always have a direct line to buy from you even if your books are not available in other online stores.

We won't go into the details of how to set these up here, for there are tutorials on how to do this.

Suffice it to say that if you are publishing independently, you should eventually set up direct sales as a safety net.

. . .

Tip: You can use a service like Book Funnel in conjunction with Selz or Payhip to deliver e-book files and handle any technological questions buyers might have about downloading files onto their devices. Book Funnel is an excellent service for this, and it can also be used to give free copies of your work to your followers.

PART IV

MARKETING

INTRODUCTION

Your book has been published traditionally or independently and is available around the world. You feel a thrill at having crossed another Rubicon. It's another victory!

But now what?

You need to market your book.

This may sound like a death knell to your creative side, but marketing can be a very creative endeavour, and a lot of fun.

It is also essential if you want to sell copies of your book in today's vast market.

As we have said before, there is more opportunity than ever for authors, but there is also a lot more noise. The online world is chaotic and crowded. You need ways to make you and your book stand out so that your readers can find you. You need to recruit new troops to your legions!

How do you do this?

Marketing.

It has been said by many that the best marketing is writing your next book. That is true to an extent. If you want a career as a historical novelist, you need something for your readers to buy after they've read your first book, and so on and so forth, so that they stay with you. Also, the more you write, the better you get at it.

However, there are other aspects to marketing that are just as effective, perhaps more so.

In this section you will learn what is essential for marketing your book, and what is not. You will also learn some tips and tricks that can help you get to #1 in the book charts.

You are the general of your marketing campaign, and your troops are ready to march once again. You need to share your common passion with them. You need to connect with them. Do that, and they will follow you anywhere.

53

Your Author Platform

IF YOU ARE TO MARKET EFFECTIVELY AND FIND YOUR true fans out there in the vast wilds of the Internet, you need to have a theme for yourself and your business as an author of historical novels.

This is your 'author platform'.

If you can, decide on this early on. Here are some questions that can help:

- What are your credentials?

- What makes you special and able to write historical fiction or historical fantasy?
- Are you a historian who is writing accurate historical fiction?
- Are you a re-enactor with a vast knowledge of the period about which you are writing?
- Are you an enthusiast for a particular period who has had a life-long passion for history and are keen to share it through your fiction?
- Have you won a short story competition with a history-themed piece of work?
- Are you a world traveller with a penchant for history?
- Are you a history-themed game designer, or a high school history teacher?

There are many possibilities.

As the inscription read upon the walls of the temple of Apollo at Delphi, 'Know Thyself'.

Think about who you are and why people should buy your book and follow you. If you've finished your book, and you love history, you are qualified.

Think about the characteristics of those qualifications. You don't need to be an academic to be qualified.

Once you have an author platform - a theme for your books and author career - then you have some solid ground on which to build your marketing campaign.

54

All Roads Lead to Your Website

In the Roman Empire, it was said that 'all roads lead to Rome'.

For you as a book marketer, all roads need to lead to your website. This is crucial.

If you don't yet have a website for yourself, your books, or your author/publisher business, you need to build one.

This has never been easier as there are free tutorials online that show you how to do this step-by-step. You no longer need to know coding to be able to build a website. You can actually build one in a very short amount of time.

Websites are the new business card.

Why do you need one?

You must have a hub, a base of operations for your marketing campaign. Almost everything you do in your marketing should lead back to your website.

Your website should contain:

- Information about you as an author, your company or series.
- A blog for regular updates on everything related to you and your books (more on blogging later).
- A bookstore with links to where people can buy your books in major online stores as well as buy direct from you.
- A free download page; and
- Perhaps most importantly, a mailing list sign-up page.

If you plan to sell in Europe (which you should) you will also need a Privacy Policy to fulfill GDPR legislation requirements. Some other extras for your website might also include excerpts of your books, a list of upcoming releases, Book Club Guides, a Pay Pal donation button (yes, this works) and more. Get creative with your website. Make it yours.

When building your own website, do not do so on a platform others own. You should own your own domain so that no one else has the ability or power to tear it down. You don't want the Carthaginians burning Rome, right? If you build your website on a free platform (e.g. Blogger) then someone else owns your website.

You need to keep your hub safe, and that means owning your domain. This information is included in the various website building tutorials you will find online.

The website you build for yourself should be interesting and fun to look at. It should be on-theme with your author platform and have lots of pictures. Too much text can turn people off. You should pick a website template that is mobile phone friendly as most people around the world are more likely to be using their phones than any other devices.

For your website, you will need to create a header image with a logo that is eye-catching. Once you have this image (you can work with a graphic designer if you can't do this yourself), you can use it wherever you have a presence online, such as on social media platforms. You want your header image to be recognizable, to be uniquely yours.

Once you have built your website and have a list of books that you are selling, you can change things up a bit and have separate tabs on your site for different series or genres.

Basically, don't overcrowd your website. Make it easy for visitors to navigate and find what they are looking for. Make your hub interesting for them to visit, so much so that they want to stay or come back, and those that do, just may become your true fans.

Tip: There are many free courses for building a website online, some geared toward authors. A good place to start is the free course offered by Joanna Penn on The Creative Penn website.

55

The Mailing List

THIS IS PERHAPS THE MOST CRUCIAL THING YOU CAN have as part of your marketing as an author of historical novels (or any novels!).

It is very important, especially if you are an independent author/publisher, because you want to have direct contact with your fans and followers. These people buy your books.

Why is it important?

When people buy your books from Amazon, Apple, Kobo, Google Play or some other store online, those companies don't tell you who has bought your books. They keep that information to themselves. They know how valuable an e-mail address and name are.

A person's e-mail address and name are personal. It provides you with direct contact to them as an individual.

The best thing you can do is collect e-mails (names are a bonus) so that, if the worst should happen, like an online store closing or blocking you as a seller, you need a way to stay in touch with your readers, to contact them on your own.

You should have a mailing list sign-up form in many places so that visitors to your website, or readers of your books, can find it easily.

There are many e-mail list service providers out there. Mailchimp and Aweber are just a couple.

Whichever one you choose, make sure it is the right fit for you. If you are not too techie, pick one that is easy to use. Think about your goals. Do you want automation such as an auto-responder sequence that sends a series of automatic emails over time to people who sign-up? Do you want detailed reports and analytics? Do you want the ability to easily segment lists so that you have separate mailing lists for different book series, or for fiction and non-fiction? There are lots of bells and whistles to various services, so you need to find what will work for you as an author and publisher.

Once you have people signing up for your list, remember to download the spreadsheet of your contacts regularly (weekly or monthly, depending on how frequently people sign-up), and keep a copy of it on your hard drive or elsewhere.

Also, keep an eye on your list. Often, people will sign-up for a mailing list but never open the e-mails. The e-mail list service provider will give you statistics that show this. Be sure to delete followers who don't open your e-mails.

And don't worry about it when people unsubscribe. This is normal. If they do unsubscribe, that means they are not your true fans. You don't need them taking up space on your list, especially if you are using a service that charges you more the larger your list gets.

It may start slowly at first, with very few people signing up to your list, but over time, it will grow. Be patient and treat your followers well.

This leads us to a question: How often should you e-mail your followers and what do you e-mail them about?

This really depends on your own style and how much work you are able to put into it. You don't want to e-mail people too frequently so that they get annoyed and unsubscribe, but you also don't want to e-mail them so little that they forget about you and your books. You have to find what works for you and your audience, and that may require some experimentation. For me, as an author, I've found that e-mailing weekly or every two weeks works well.

But what do you e-mail your followers about?

Authors seem to find this complicated, but it really is easy. E-mails don't have to be long diatribes that people never read to the end. They can be short and informative. They should be interesting.

Some examples of what you can e-mail your list about are:

- new blog posts
- new releases
- personal news related to your writing or research; and
- special offers

Always remember to adapt the subject line of the e-mail to the content within. For example, if you are telling your followers about a special offer, be sure to put something like 'Time-sensitive Special Offer' in the subject line of the e-mail.

At this point, you may be asking yourself 'How can I get people to sign-up to my mailing list?'

That is an excellent question, and the answer is that you need something called a 'lead magnet', something they receive for free in return for them giving you their personal e-mail. More on this in the next chapter.

Basically, when dealing with your mailing list subscribers, a good general rule for everything you send them is that whatever it is, it should surprise and delight them. If you do that, they will stick with you for the long-haul.

Tip: Put your mailing list sign-up form everywhere possible such as at the front and back of your books, the sidebar of your website using a plug-in, a full page of your website, advertisements on social media, and website pop-ups (yes, these work!). Make that mailing list sign-up highly visible so that every visitor to your site, and reader of your books, sees it. You will have a growing list of followers in no time!

56

Lead Magnets

BEFORE POTENTIAL READERS OF YOUR WORK CAN become followers, they will be mercenaries. You need to give them an incentive to join your ranks. You need to make it worth their while. You don't need to be a war leader with bags of gold to do this, but you do need a lead magnet.

The lead magnet is one of your most important marketing tools, and you definitely need to have one if you expect people to sign-up for your mailing list and give you their personal e-mail which, as we have said, is very valuable.

The lead magnet is an incentive, something you give a person for free for signing-up for your mailing list.

What sorts of lead magnets can a historical author give that are tempting enough for someone to hand over their email?

Well, the best thing is a free book that is related to your historical fiction or historical fantasy novel. Ideally, it could be the first in a series, or a prequel, something to pull readers into the world you have created.

If you don't want to give away a full novel, or if you only have one novel, try writing a short story or novella related to the series or at least to the period of history your story takes place in. Some authors give away PDFs of a map of their book's world, but this would work more if you are already established. No one really wants a map to a world they are not familiar with. Perhaps a PDF or short e-book with information on the historical period? Remember, you want to connect with people through your common love of history. You could put together something with information on the weapons of the period, the clothing, social mores etc. Whatever it is, make it something that is related to the story, or the history, and make it interesting. Get creative and think outside of the dungeon!

You need to tempt people, to draw them in. Whatever lead magnet you come up with, make sure you blog about it and promote it so that the word can get out that a new war leader is in town, and that he or she is offering gold!

You won't keep all of those followers who sign-up, but many will become loyal and stick with you for the long march.

Tip: If you create a new lead magnet at any point in time, be sure to give it to your current followers as a sort of 'Thank You'. They will feel appreciated and it will reinforce their decision to have started following you.

57

Blogging is Your Secret Weapon!

All right. Now we come to it. Listen carefully…

Word on the street is that blogging is dead or ineffective. You will hear this a lot, but I am here to tell you that this is not true at all.

As part of your ongoing marketing for your books and you as an author, blogging is your secret weapon, but only if it is done right. It is part of your content marketing and can leave a very long trail on the vast plain of the Internet that leads back to you and your website.

Blogging does many things for the historical novelist:

- Creates an evergreen backlog of content that will constantly lead people back to your website and books. Every blog is like a century of troops sent out into the world
- Establishes and solidifies your authority on your subject matter, and supports your author platform
- It is a regular way, and a good excuse, to make contact with your readers so that they remember and appreciate you between novels
- Keeps your own head in the world of your books
- Keeps you writing and honing your skills
- Gives you more content that you can publish and sell later (remember the book and movie, *Julie and Julia*? Well, that started as a blog - not historical, but a good example).

This very book you are reading came about as a result of ten years of blogging and experience in content marketing. Because of the *Writing the Past* blog, researchers, novelists, hobbyists and other people have come to me, and to Eagles and Dragons Publishing, for more information and advice on a wide range of topics, or to thank us, because of our blog and the years of content.

It really hit home how powerful and important blogging can be when a New York casting agent for the History Channel contacted me to see if I was interested in auditioning to host a television show on ancient ingenuity. It didn't pan out, but I did do the audition, getting way out of my comfort zone! I did manage to ask the casting agent how they found out about me, and she said that it was through my books and - wait for it - my blog. She said they wanted someone with authority on the subject matter.

That really showed me the power of blogging.

Had I not been blogging, that opportunity would never have presented itself. Now, not all of us want to be television show hosts (I certainly wasn't sure I wanted to!), but we do want the regular exposure that blogging can give us.

I know, I know... Many of you are wondering

what on earth you could blog about, and how often do you have to do it?

The frequency of your blogging is up to you and your routine, but it should be often enough that your readers and followers don't forget about you. I've found that blogging weekly or every two weeks works well for me and for my followers. Whatever blogging schedule you decide on, be consistent and regular if you can.

What you, as a historical novelist, can blog about is important and here is the key: everything you blog about should be related to your books, your chosen period of history, and your author platform.

This sounds restrictive, but it is not for the historical novelist. Here are some examples about what you could blog about:

- Your research for your books
- Any aspect of everyday life during your historical period and culture (dining in ancient Rome, for example)
- Artifacts from the period or culture
- Social mores and norms of that culture
- Specific weapons or military units
- Major historical events that take place

during the historical period and/or the period covered by your book. If it is fantasy, perhaps you have historical events that inspired the book?
- Recent discoveries related to your period of history
- Travel to sites that are featured in your book

Basically, as long as it relates to your book and your chosen historical period in some way, you can blog about it. It really is wide open!

Lastly, there is one more very important thing that blogging can do for you as an author and publisher: it will help you sell books.

With regular blogging, I've noticed, over time, that every time I post a blog and share it with my mailing list and on social media platforms, there is almost always a visible spike in books sales.

That is your secret weapon at work!

Tip: For every book you release, create a blog series around that specific book. Make it at least a five-part series and release it over the weeks after your book launch. This will help you to maintain the launch momentum and keep sales going. It will also go a long way to helping you rank in the charts for your category. Link to this blog series in the back of the book and on the book's sales page on your website.

58

Social Media

Many people either love or hate social media, it's true, and social media is a potential labyrinth of wasted time for authors. But, it can be one of the best, most affordable tools for spreading the word about your books, blog, and other content.

How do you determine which social media platforms to use to market your books, yourself, and your company? This is a tough question because social media is changing all the time. New platforms emerge and others lose their influence or significance. How do you decide? There are two questions you can ask yourself:

- Who are my ideal readers, my audience?
- Where are they hanging out online?

At the moment (late 2019), Facebook seems to be more for older readers, whereas something like Snapchat is for a much younger crowd. And this will change as new platforms emerge. Whenever you are reading this book, you will need to take a close look at what social media looks like for you, and ascertain which platforms your ideal readers are using.

Currently, at the time of publication, Eagles and Dragons Publishing has found that Facebook, Instagram, and Twitter are effective, but that could change at any moment. It could no longer be true by the time you read this.

If you have not started marketing your books yet, pick one social media platform to focus on. See how it works for a while. If you get results, stick with it. If it doesn't work for you, try another platform until you find one that does.

For many, social media can be a burden. It can be

toxic. One of the keys to social media is that you pick one you enjoy using, because if you don't, it will show.

Once you decide on a social media platform you want to use, you will encounter a level of toxic behaviour. You will have to fight trolls on the march.

The truth is that the more success you have, the more trolls will come out.

Don't engage them! Always take the higher ground, because anything you say or do will come back at you. And don't get political! You could end up neglecting some of your readers.

There is one instance in which you should consider engaging a troll online and that is when they are saying things that could hurt your author platform or discredit you. This happened to me once when someone commented on something I wrote about the temple of Apollo in Rome on the Palatine Hill. The person accused me of not knowing that Apollo was a Greek god, and not Roman. I saw that a few people were following the interaction, so I felt compelled to set the person straight.

After a few deep breaths, I calmly pointed out the facts that both the Greeks and Romans worshiped Apollo, and that the temple on the Palatine Hill in Rome was built by Emperor Augustus. I also provided a link to an official website backing this up. This particular troll stopped his behaviour, especially when other people started agreeing with the facts I had presented.

The key to this small engagement was to remain polite (even if the troll was not), respectful, and to answer with facts. It reinforced my authority on the subject.

Now, if a troll persists in their attacks, you can block them. You don't need that negativity or stress, and neither do your readers.

Another aspect of social media that works very well for marketing your books and you as an author are Facebook groups for history, archaeology, historical fiction and anything else related to your period of history.

Find these groups, join them. Participate and interact in discussions. Start discussions, and share other people's posts in those groups. Just don't try to sell.

This sounds strange, true. Join groups to sell books, but don't *sell* books?

Many groups on social media platforms like Facebook have strict rules about self-promotion. Most of the time, you can't share anything about your books, but you absolutely can share every blog post you write about the history related to your books!

By sharing your blogs, which in turn display your knowledge of the subject matter, people will end up visiting your website where they will also see your books, your mailing list sign-up and everything else. You don't even need to mention your books.

Eagles and Dragons Publishing has noticed a definite spike in sales and new mailing list subscribers every time a blog is posted or shared in Facebook Groups.

The bottom line is, enjoy interacting with (not selling to) like-minded people online and it will pay off.

59

Who to Market to

Marketing can be daunting for many people. It can be a steep learning curve. And knowing who to market to is important so that you don't waste time and money.

You often hear about the 'ideal reader'. We mentioned that in the previous chapter.

Think about it for a few moments. Who is your ideal reader? What are their interests and reading habits?

This is important because you need to know

where to direct your marketing efforts, and who to target.

For historical fiction and historical fantasy, you don't necessarily want to target other writers. They may not be your ideal readers. In fact, they probably are not.

So, how do you determine who your ideal readers are? The deeper you can dig into this, the more effective your marketing efforts will be. Here are some questions to help you develop a profile of your ideal reader:

- What type of fiction is your historical novel? Is it academic or romantic? Is it adventure? Is it more history or more fantasy?
- Are your readers history fanatics or casual readers?
- What age group is best suited to your novel?
- What sex? Would men or women prefer your books? Both?
- What are their habits? Do they travel? Are they interested in the details you give in your novels?

- What are the potential reading habits of your ideal reader? If they are binge readers, can you produce books often enough to keep them happy?
- Are they members of book clubs?

Once you have a general picture of your ideal reader, find out where they are online. For example, re-enactor groups are passionate hobbyists who may be potential readers, and many of these folks have social media groups.

Do some searching and find where potential ideal readers may be, and get to know them without selling to them. You won't hit the mark every time, but you will narrow things down until the picture of your ideal reader is much more clear.

Remember, you are not marketing to your friends and family. You are marketing to your ideal readers who are passionate about your period of history and who read fiction.

Tip: Once you have a following of subscribers, survey them to find out who they are and what their preferences and interests are. This will help you to develop a clear picture of your ideal reader.

60

The Importance of Advertising

This is a difficult subject for most introverted authors. Marketing is tough enough, but to add advertising on top of it, well… You would rather be writing, wouldn't you?

But if you want to make a living writing and selling books, you need to up your game and advertise. At this moment in the publishing industry, advertising in the right places will be for you as the invention of the stirrup or Spanish steel were to the warrior classes of Medieval Europe.

Advertising will give you a definite edge and boost your books sales.

In the crowded, online marketplace, it is essential that you advertise, especially as many online stores or social media platforms require that you 'pay to play' if you want your books or posts to get in front of people's eyes.

Yes, it is upsetting, and yes, it is absolutely necessary.

You need to set aside a budget for advertising, even if it is only $50 per month. And where do you place these ads? Well, there are opportunities to advertise everywhere on various social media platforms and online stores. There are even services that will run advertising for you.

However, you need to be cautious. Advertising can suck up your budget very quickly with little to show for it. You need to decide where is the best, most effective place to advertise. This will, of course, change over time as the online world is always in flux, but at the moment there are a few places where ads can help boost book sales the most:

- Amazon Ads - each country is separate and requires a different ad account, but this is very effective in boosting sales on Amazon. You can target specific keywords (hundreds) as well that are specific to your book.

- Book Bub Ads - Book Bub is the biggest discount book mailing list service and as a result can be one of the most effective platforms to advertise on. It is also one of the most expensive, but that is for a good reason. If you can afford Book Bub ads, then there is a market of enthusiastic readers looking for deals on fiction.

- Mailing list Services - there are many services that have lists of genre-specific readers who receive daily e-mails about deals for fiction and non-fiction, too many to list here. However, at the moment services like Bargain Booksy, Free Booksy, Kindle Nation Daily and several others will place your book in an e-mail for a fee. If you use these service correctly, they could boost your book's sales ranking around the time of a launch or a special promotion you are running.

- Facebook Ads - advertising on the world's biggest social media platform can be frustrating and very expensive. It is complicated to say the least. That said, if you can figure it out and hone the targeting of your ads (age, sex, interests, habits etc.) you could, quite literally, make millions. But you need to spend money to make money on this platform, and Facebook makes it very easy for advertisers to spend money. This really took off when Facebook decided that users had to 'boost' posts in order for more of their followers to see them. Again, you have to 'pay to play' on Facebook. If you do try Facebook ads, start with a low budget and experiment with ad copy and images to find the right combination with your chosen targeting options.

These are just a few examples of where you can advertise your books. There are others of course, such as Twitter, Pinterest etc. But some may not be as effective at selling books.

Think of your own ideal readers and where they are online. If there are advertising opportunities in those places, you may want to try them. Also, think of your own buying and social media habits. Where do you click on ads? Do you click on them at all? What usually catches your attention? All of this is useful information.

Advertising can cost a lot of money with an unknown ROI (Return on Investment), so it requires care, attention to detail, and experimentation with ad copy, photos and more until you find the right formula. Remember to start with a low budget and see what works and what doesn't. Check your ads daily to see how they are performing.

If you can nail ads, you will be laughing all the way to the vaults of your fortress!

Tip: There are many ad courses for authors out there, such as Mark Dawson's *Ads for Authors* course. Take some of the free webinars and then consider investing in the full course. Investing time and money in this sort of training has changed many an author's life. Remember, advertising is essential to making a good income selling books online.

61

Using Photos

The importance of using photos in everything you do as part of your marketing cannot be overstated. online, people are visual and have short attention spans.

Think about it. Do you ever click on a social media or other post that does not have a photo? Unless you are looking for a very specific answer to a question or problem, you probably don't even give it a second glance. If something does not have images, most people just pass right on by.

Photos are attractive and can tell a 'story' or get a message across in a matter of seconds.

That is why you should use photos in everything you do from ads to blog posts, to shared items or social media posts. Put photos everywhere!

Where can you get photos? There are a few places.

Use photos you have taken yourself on your travels over the years, especially photos of sites related to the history of your book. These photos don't just have to be for research, they can be used for ads, blog posts and more.

Pay for a membership with one of the many online stock photo companies. Big advertising and other media companies use these. Find one that has high quality images that fit the theme of what you are looking for (pictures of ancient sites or castles, for example).

Use royalty-free images from online sources such as Pixabay or Wikimedia Commons. Often these images are of lesser quality, or have been used by others, but they can still be effective. Be careful to look up the usage rights, as some photos don't allow manipulation for commercial purposes.

Once you find images that you would like to use, and if the rights for those images allow it, you may wish to manipulate them for your purposes. You can do this for free on sites like Canva or PIXLR.

Remember, if you use a photo that was taken by someone else for a blog post or ad, you need to get permission to do so and provide an attribution. This will protect you from potential copyright breach and legal action.

Develop a common style to everything you do so that you and your brand have a familiar feel, font etc. Branding is important when it comes to marketing.

Most of all, when it comes to sharing your work and playing with photos, be sure to have fun and share your passion. It could make the difference between an ad or blog post people skip over or one that they click on and share.

Tip: Develop special headers with images for each blog series you write. This will make it immediately recognizable to your followers or potential customers on social media platforms.

62

Video

If photos are your front line troops in an engagement, then video is the heavy cavalry charge.

Video is something that many authors struggle with, especially the introverts among us. Few people like how they look and sound on video.

However, if you can bring yourself to come out of your comfort zone and try using video more and more in your social media interactions and advertising, then it will put your marketing results through the roof!

It is definitely worth trying, and the good thing is

that you don't need expensive equipment to do it these days. Most smartphones will work just fine.

But what can you film? How can authors of historical novels make use of video to sell books and promote themselves? Everyone is different, but some ways in which you can use video are:

- Short, informal social media posts about new releases or updates for followers
- Videos of visits to historical sites you are researching
- Short documentaries of visits to sites, combined with photos, and put together in a program like iMovie. These will draw readers farther into the world of your novels!
- A short video of you reading an excerpt from your novel

Because so few authors do use video, it has the potential to make you stand out even more. Remember, if you do create a video, post it on your website and on social media, and link to relevant videos in the back of your books.

If you can make effective use of video, there will be little to stop you.

Tip: If your book is done first, but you plan to do a video or documentary later, in the back of the book put a link to a page on your website that says 'Coming Soon'. When the video is finished, update that page of your website.

63

Repurposing Content

THE CONTENT THAT YOU HAVE CREATED OVER TIME will accumulate. After ten years of blog posts on *Writing the Past*, there is a lot of content there. The same will occur for your blog, the videos you create, the photos you take, and the short fiction you write.

When it comes to content marketing, you don't want to share a blog post or other piece of content just once and then forget about it.

When it comes to posts about history, research, site visits and other things you have gone to the trouble of creating, you should repurpose and re-use them. Much of this will be evergreen content, so share it again and again. You will be getting new followers all the time, and many of them will not have seen older content.

You can also repurpose content for articles for publications, guest blog posts on other websites, or even to create a separate book.

Look at the content you have created over time and see what can be re-shared and repurposed. You might be surprised by some of your older work!

Tip: When you re-share older blog posts on social media, remember to change up the copy and images from previous uses. Watch for current or new discoveries or films related to that content and update as needed. A share content related to your own content. There is such a thing as 'good karma' on social media!

64

Network Like Caesar!

To many, 'networking' is a dirty word that conjures images of sly grins and sweaty handshakes. It is often difficult for writers to come out of their shells and go out into the world.

But it is important to do so. You need to network.

Don't be afraid to meet people at conferences, or to undertake group work, collaborations, do guest blogs or interviews on other sites.

Networking with other writers or bloggers in your genre can help you to tap into new audiences. This includes e-mailing or connecting with others on social media.

Networking can be daunting, terrifying even, but it can have some surprising results like a blurb for your book from a respected author in your genre, or an interview on a podcast that increases your following or sales.

Get out into the forum of the world like Julius Caesar, and shake some hands. You never know what might happen, his end notwithstanding!

65

Be Consistent, Be Present

THERE IS A LOT OF NOISE ONLINE, AND THAT MEANS that readers and potential buyers of your books are easily distracted.

Consistency and presence are important aspects of your book marketing.

You cannot place one ad or send one e-mail and then expect ongoing results. You need to stay present in people's minds or you will be forgotten, especially in the beginning as you establish yourself as an author and publisher.

A few things you can do to be consistent and present in your marketing are:

- Blogging regularly
- E-mailing your followers regularly (but not too much!)
- Advertising continuously (some advertising experts say that people need to see an ad up to seven times before they take action!)
- Posting and interacting regularly on social media, including groups

Remember to be consistent in your activities and be friendly to your followers. Be present, and listen to people who spend time reading your content. They will show their appreciation in return.

Tip: Schedule all of your activities on a calendar (digital or paper) and check them off as you go. Schedule a couple of marketing tasks per day - no more - always allowing time for your writing and editing. This will help you feel accomplished and avoid overwhelm.

66

Be Adventurous

Many of the great people in history were not afraid of change, or if they were, they did not let fear of change hold them back. They jumped right in!

Rapid change, such as what the book industry is experiencing, means that there are always new opportunities in publishing and marketing books.

A lot of writers who try something new early on, often find big success, even if they fail a few times at first.

When you are looking for ways to market your books, be adventurous.

Do not be afraid to try new things, to experiment. Get out of your comfort zone.

When new opportunities are available, it is often the early adopters who find the most success.

Tip: Try something new every month. When you find something that works, that gets you positive results, stick with it until it doesn't.

67

Reinforcements

Over time, as you develop a loyal following, you may want to recruit people whom you can call upon should the need arise. You will want what many call a 'street team'.

What is a 'street team'? Well, it's not a gang of Suburan street thugs carrying cudgels and trying to sway votes in an upcoming election. A 'street team' is a group of your biggest fans and supporters who will help spread the word about your books, post reviews of your books, share posts, be beta readers for you, and generally support all of your marketing efforts.

These are important people, and they can make a huge difference in your marketing.

Take care of these folks by doing some of the following:

- Give them copies of your books
- Connect with them
- Create a special forum (like a secret Facebook Group) where you can interact with them
- Send them merchandise for themselves and to share so they can help spread the word (bookmarks or post cards are good for this)
- Put on an event! Some of the very successful authors even hold events or retreats for their greatest supporters

Get creative and show your appreciation for the people who support you and your marketing efforts. Your street team may grow slowly, but over time you will have a force of loyal fans whom you can call upon in time of need.

68

Crowdsourcing

This is something that has become quite popular in recent years for many creative people. Sometimes, you have a project that you are dying to do or finish, but you just don't have the capital to make it happen. That sounds familiar, doesn't it?

Crowdsourcing has become a popular way for artists and other creatives to raise money for a specific project by asking for one-time donations to support that project, and then rewarding donors with something related to it.

This is done through online platforms such as Kickstarter and GoFundMe.

For authors of historical novels, this can be a new series of professional book covers, the creation of proper maps, the filming of a high-quality documentary etc. It is not intended to fund your vacation abroad where you can do a little research and then relax the rest of the time.

Crowdsourcing can be extremely helpful. But there is a catch!

For crowdsourcing to work, you need an established following, or a product that people feel the world (or themselves) really needs.

No one is going to give money to an author they don't know so that they can create cool maps for books they are not familiar with.

If you are not yet a world-famous scribe with tens of thousands of followers, you may not be ready for crowdsourcing. You may want to go the route of ongoing patronage instead!

69

Patronage

PATRONAGE OF ARTISTS IS A LONGSTANDING tradition. William Shakespeare had Queen Elizabeth I as his patron, and Michelangelo had the Pope! You're in good company here.

Today, there is a resurgence in patronage of artists, including authors. Having a patronage option available will allow your super fans to support you.

How and where can you do this?

Sites and services like Patreon allow any artist to collect patrons and receive ongoing, monthly payments from them. This is done in exchange for various rewards, depending on the level of patronage. This can provide an author with a monthly income, and several authors have been able to make a full-time income from their patrons alone.

That is exciting!

Again, you need a following to embark on this, and you need to think long-term. Gathering a group of patrons who will support you and your work does not happen overnight. But over time, as more and more people decide to join your patron group, you will be surprised and grateful at the contributions.

If you do start gathering patrons to your artistic cause, be sure to treat them extremely well. These are your most important and loyal followers. Provide exciting rewards for each level of patronage, and show your appreciation. Answer their questions or e-mails right away. Make them a priority. Even $1.00 per month patrons give you $12.00 per year. That's more than the price of a couple of e-books for most independent authors!

Give your patrons first looks, sneak peeks and other bonuses. Write short stories, just for them. Acknowledge them by name at the end of your books. There is a lot you can do to show your appreciation, and if you do, they will remain your patrons for the long term.

. . .

Tip: Before setting up a Patreon account, create a clear plan of goals and rewards that you are able to deliver on. Make sure you have enough patronage levels to allow for some choice, but not too many so that a potential patron get overwhelmed and turns away. If you want to take a look at the Eagles and Dragons Publishing Patreon page, to see how it is set up, you can check it out here:

https://www.patreon.com/EaglesandDragonsPublishing

70

Timing is Everything

SUCCESSFUL GENERALS KNOW WHEN TO MAKE THEIR crucial move in a battle or campaign, so they can snatch victory and win the war. The same, in a way, goes for your book marketing.

The more you learn about marketing and your own efforts over time, the more you will notice patterns and be able to anticipate things.

You need to be aware of the highs and lows of the calendar year as far as book sales, and plan accordingly. Don't forget holidays like Christmas, or events like Black Friday and Cyber Monday. Don't forget back to school, Father's Day, or Mother's Day, when books are purchased for class or as gifts.

At certain times of year, when people are primed and ready to shop and spend money, you, as a general, need to be ready to strike. Run a promotion or special offer during these periods, have a box set sale. Do something to mark the occasion and tempt would-be customers.

But just as you need to be aware of the big selling times of year, you also need to be aware of the lull periods such as July and August when people have already bought their summer reading. Try to counter the lull period with special offers, and be sure to advertise these offers.

Plan accordingly for possible financial shortfalls at certain times of year so that you can make your own crucial move to counter it.

With the highs and lows in book sales during the year, timing is everything!

Tip: Historical novelists have an advantage when it comes to enthusiasts for their chosen period of history. You can create special offers around holidays from your particular period in history. For example, the ancient Romans celebrated the *Feriae Marti* on the first of March, which coincided with the birthday of the god Mars. If you write Roman war novels, you could run a short promotion or sale on this day. History is vast, and the sky's the limit. Think about your period of history and how you can turn old holidays into an interesting marketing opportunity.

BONUS SECTION

MINDSET

INTRODUCTION

At this point, you've learned a lot about researching, writing, publishing and marketing historical fiction and historical fantasy. The opportunities for authors and publishers today are extremely exciting, but despite this 'new world' of publishing, there is a distinct possibility of overwhelm. Many authors have burned out, some of them stopping writing altogether.

For creative people in business, including authors, mindset is extremely important if you are to weather the storms ahead.

In this bonus section, you will learn about some of the pitfalls of writing and publishing and the relevant mindset tips to help you stay strong, keep on marching, and keep on writing.

You can do this.

1

Avoid 'Comparisonitis'

EVERY HERO'S JOURNEY IS UNIQUE, AND SO IS EVERY writer's.

Constantly comparing yourself to other authors and publishers and their successes (#of books published, #of sales, income etc.) can not only be depressing, but also crippling. Comparing yourself needlessly with others can prevent you from doing the work you need to do, that you were meant to do.

Focus on *your* task and *your* work, and you will achieve your goals.

Odysseus did not wonder how Menelaus was

doing on his way back from Troy with Helen. He thought of reaching Ithaca and nothing else.

Don't worry about other authors and their journeys.

Focus on your own journey and, in time, you will achieve your goals.

2

Give Yourself Permission to Suck!

ROME'S FIRST ATTEMPTS AT WAR WERE TERRIBLE, BUT they kept on fighting, training, and learning. Eventually, they became the best army of the ancient world.

The same goes for authors. No writer is excellent in their first attempt, but with learning, training and more writing, you improve.

Give yourself permission to suck at first, whether it is your first book or the first draft of your tenth book.

If you give yourself permission to not be perfect,

you will free yourself from unreal expectation and numbing self-doubt.

My writing mentor's advice is important here: *Just get the story down. No matter what. Get it down!*

Don't worry about editing or perfecting the first draft, just keep writing to the end and don't mind if it is awful.

Just get your story down and fix things later. After all, it's better to have a rough but complete first draft of a story than two polished chapters.

3

No Book is Perfect

HISTORICAL NOVELIST BERNARD CORNWELL ONCE told a group of us in a master class not to overedit.

He was right!

Not only should you not expect yourself to write perfectly, you should not expect your book to be perfect.

No book is perfect!

Of course, you should always do your best and get help from editors and beta readers, but after that, just let your book out into the world to experience life and grow.

4

Put Your Writing First

Presumably, the reason you got into all of this is because you love writing historical fiction or historical fantasy.

In this modern age of publishing, it is easy to get overwhelmed and freeze up. Many writers are burning out.

For this reason, you need to take care. When you, as a creative person, are feeling overwhelmed with publishing and marketing, when you are feeling stressed and worried, just stop.

Take a breath.

Go back to what you love for a time: writing stories.

Put your writing first. It feels good.

It is also productive.

If it is the writing that is bringing you down, stop that and do something else. Exercise, or refill your creative well by visiting a historic site or museum. Watch historical movies or documentaries. Walk through a forest and connect with nature.

When something is getting you down, do something else that makes you happy.

Take breaks when needed and you'll be more productive and ready to get stuck back into the melee.

5

Be a Business

After the creative writing is done, you need to get into a business mindset if you are to succeed and achieve longterm success.

Don't be precious about your work. Trust me, I know that's difficult! But it is important to let go.

Businesses make tough decisions all the time that are, in the end, good for the company. Successful businesses also fail, and then try new things.

Remember, it is good to fail because you, as an author and a business, will learn from failure in every aspect of your business of writing and publishing.

DaVinci and Beethoven failed at first, so when you too fail, and then keep trying, you are among the ranks of history's greatest creative minds!

6

Don't Give Up

Like Alexander the Great marching to the ends of the Earth, you will face many hurdles along the way, fight many battles.

People will tell you that what you are trying to do is impossible, that you can't do it.

No matter how hard it gets, how impossible it seems, or how many people try to drag you down, just keep going and you will be victorious.

When I was a teenager and decided I wanted to write historical fiction, I was told by the people closest to me that I could not be a writer or make a living from writing.

Those words hurt.

But I ignored them and kept at it. I achieved victories I had once only dreamed of, and am now a best-selling author with a loyal following.

No matter what, no matter how difficult things get, or how many people tell you you can't do this, I'm here to say that you can.

Don't give up. Victory is within your grasp!

7

Think Longterm

For sustained success, and if you want to make a living from your writing, you need to think longterm.

Writing and publishing success is a long game. Any 'overnight' or 'out-of-the-gate' successes that you have heard about are either outliers, or a romantic notion sold to writers by Hollywood and traditional publishing.

You need to be patient, focus on your campaign and do what needs to be done. If you do this, you will conquer your own part of the world.

Think longterm and you will find success.

8

Connecting Through History

AS A HISTORICAL NOVELIST, HISTORY IS IMPORTANT IN everything you do. You love history, and so do your readers.

Make this the common ground between you and your readers.

Remember to connect with your audience through your shared love of history by sharing your love, passion and enthusiasm for the subjects and historical eras you write about.

If you do this, if you connect with people through

history, you will develop strong bonds with your readers and create loyal fans.

9

Don't Worry about Pirates

ONE THING MANY AUTHORS WORRY ABOUT IN THE online world is piracy.

The truth is, however, that this is a fact of doing online business, and there is little you can do to change it.

Don't worry about the things you cannot change.

If you set about hunting down pirates like Pompey the Great did, you won't be doing any writing.

This is important: the people who get pirated books, movies, music etc., are not going to buy your books anyway. So let it be.

If someone steals your work, however, and sells it and makes a lot of money, then you should consult a lawyer about pursuing legal action.

Otherwise, don't worry about pirates.

10

Be Realistic

To avoid overwhelm and burnout, it is important to set realistic goals and expectations.

Do not make your to-do lists for the day, week, or month, overly long. Do not expect to sell millions of books or gain thousands of subscribers in a weekend.

Work to gain loyal followers and sell books one by one, and you will not be disappointed.

If you are realistic, you will quite often end up being pleasantly surprised.

11

It is OK to Lose Subscribers

ONCE YOU HAVE A MAILING LIST, YOU WILL GET people unsubscribing.

That is all right. It is even good! These are acceptable casualties in your campaign to achieve writing and publishing success.

Your mailing list should, ideally, be made up of loyal followers, true fans who love what you do. You do not want people who are not interested in buying your books or reading your blog on your mailing list. Often, you are paying to have them on that list!

When you get unsubscribes, even though it may sting a little, think of it as making room for future true fans.

12

Take Breaks

Writing and Publishing is a lot of hard work, even if you love it. Authors and publishers - especially independent ones - often work far more hours than those in a regular nine-to-five job.

You need to ensure that you take breaks to exercise, travel, or do whatever you love. You need to decompress to avoid burnout.

Take care of your physical, mental, and creative health.

If you need to, schedule breaks and time off.

Protect those time slots. You will be a better, more productive writer and publisher if you do!

13

Be Kind to Yourself

THIS IS PERHAPS THE SIMPLEST, BUT MOST IMPORTANT tip in this entire book.

It applies to all aspects of the writing and publishing journey.

We all want success in writing and publishing. We want our marketing efforts to bear fruit. But in our enthusiasm to succeed, to reach our goals and make our dreams come true, we are, more often than not, extremely harsh on ourselves.

Over time, this has a negative impact on everything we do.

Be kind to yourself.

Allow for your writing to be less than you hoped for or expected.

Allow for low sales.

Allow for failed marketing campaigns.

If you keep learning and keep trying, while being kind to yourself, you will eventually find success.

Enjoy the journey. Pursue your passion for history and writing, and in the process you will be living your own, unique, epic adventure.

BONUS SECTION

BOOK LAUNCH STRATEGY

INTRODUCTION

If you do some research online for book launch strategies, you will see myriad options and ways of doing things. There is no single, fool-proof way to successfully launch a book. There are many variables involved that can differ, depending on the genre, audience, and the habits of that audience.

You need to find a launch strategy that works for you and your books, and this will take some experimentation. That said, there are certain things you can do that are proven to work for most authors.

In this special bonus section, Eagles and Dragons Publishing is going to share with you the basic launch strategy that we have developed over time and that has earned us four #1 bestselling titles, as well as other bestseller labels, in fiction and non-fiction.

At this point, it is assumed that you have the following things in place before you try out this launch strategy:

- A finished, well-edited book
- An eye-catching, genre-specific book cover
- A good book description or blurb
- An author or publisher website to direct people to
- A decent-sized mailing list of followers (say, over 200 active followers)
- E-book and paperback files that have been finalized and are ready to go

Some parts of this strategy are easily customizable so that it fits your style, but if you are going to try it, don't veer too far off the path. This strategy has worked well for Eagles and Dragons Publishing. It could work just as well, or better, for you.

Let's get started…

Eagles and Dragons Publishing

Book Launch Strategy for Historical Fiction and Historical Fantasy

1) Build Excitement - you want to get your followers excited about your upcoming book release. Give hints about what is coming, including a 'special offer' just for them.

2) Upload your book files - simultaneously upload all of your book files to the sites you publish on. This should include your e-book, paperback and hardcover book, audio-books, and any other format files you may have. Make them all available and ready for people to buy online.

3) Set a low price - you want to set the initial price lower than it will be, and then notify your mailing list of followers that the e-book (only the e-book!) is discounted just for them, and only for 3 days. Don't advertise this lower price to anyone but your followers. Make them feel special, because they are! Tell your followers on your mailing list that they should get their copies for the lower price while they can!

Mark the e-mail you send them as 'Time Sensitive Offer' in the subject line of the e-mail.

How much should you discount? That depends on you, but you need to make the price too good for people to pass up! For example, if the regular price of your new e-book is going to be $4.99, you could make the three-day, discounted price for your followers $0.99.

Important: Check your rankings in the online stores and take screen shots of your book in high rankings in different categories, especially if you get a #1 Bestseller label in a particular category. You can use these screen shots in marketing and social media later.

4) Raise the price of your book - after the three days at the discounted, launch price for followers, raise the price to the regular price you planned on using. Once the pricing changes have taken effect in all the stores where your book is available, you are ready for your 'official' launch.

5) Announce your new book to the world - it is time for the official launch of your book. Announce it everywhere you can. Send another e-mail to your followers thanking them for their help (tell them if it reached a high ranking!). Write a blog announcing the new book that includes the cover and full book description, as well as links to all the places people can buy it, whether through our own website or to individual stores. Share this blog with punchy copy across all the social media platforms, and be sure to use attractive pictures and even some of the screen shots of your new book in top ranking positions. Lay it all out there and spread the word. Ask your online friends to help you.

6) Keep up the launch momentum - to maintain the momentum of a launch, this is when you can launch your blog series about the research that went into your novel. The purpose is to draw readers further into the world of your novel and keep your new release present in people's minds until they buy a copy. Remember, history is your shared passion with your readers.

Share every blog post with your mailing list followers, your patrons if you have any, and across all social media groups (this is where your participation in those history-themed Facebook groups will pay off!).

Remember to use interesting copy and graphics or pictures with each post. The blog series should be at least five posts long, and released on a weekly (or bi-weekly) basis. Every post should have the book cover at the end, as well as the links to read more about it and buy the book, ideally on the book's web page on your own website.

When sharing these blog posts on social media groups, do NOT mention the book. Most groups don't like self-promotion. History is your connection point. Just mention the subject of the post (Hadrian's Wall, for example), and you'll get positive attention.

7) Advertise - once your new book is out, and people are buying it, you have to advertise to get more eyes on it. Use Amazon, Facebook, Book Bub ads and others during this launch period, especially if it is a first in series.

You can also advertise the first in series simultaneously if the new book is a later volume in the series. Be sure to watch for screen shot opportunities during any advertising campaign.

That's all there is to it. These seven steps should give you and your book a good start!

Remember, you can customize some of these steps and draw things out over a longer period of time (try a ten-part blog series about the world of your book!).

In tandem with the steps above, you can also add guest blogs and interview opportunities on podcasts to the mix. Get creative!

Of course there are never any guarantees, but it has worked for Eagles and Dragons Publishing several times. It could work for you!

Now… Your legions are mustered, you trained hard and are ready to work to conquer the dreams you've had for so long.

You can do this.

Good luck!

Thank you for reading!

Did you find *Writing the Past* helpful? Here is what you can do next.

If you found this Eagles and Dragons Publishing Guide helpful in your work or aspirations as a historical novelist, and if you have a minute to spare, please post a short review on the web page where you purchased this book.

Reviews are a wonderful way for other historical novelists to find this book, and your help in spreading the word is greatly appreciated.

If you would like to join Eagles and Dragons Publishing's Masters of Historical Fiction and Historical Fantasy community, just visit the link below:

https://eaglesanddragonspublishing.com/eagles-and-dragons-publishing-masters-of-historical-fiction-and-historical-fantasy/

Members get a FREE PDF of the Historical Novel Book Launch Strategy Blueprint, and first access to new releases, special offers, and much more!

Authors who need a bit of extra help on their publishing journey can also check out Eagles and Dragons Publishing's consulting and author-coaching services here:

https://eaglesanddragonspublishing.com/consulting-author-coaching/

Become a Patron of Eagles and Dragons Publishing!

If you enjoy the books that Eagles and Dragons Publishing puts out, our blogs about history, mythology, and archaeology, our video tours of historic sites, author training and more, then you should consider becoming an official patron.

We love our regular visitors to the website, and of course our wonderful newsletter subscribers, but we want to offer more to our 'super fans', those readers and history-lovers who enjoy everything we do and create.

You can become a patron for as little as $1 per month. For your support, you will also get loads of fantastic rewards as tokens of our appreciation.

If you are interested, visit the website below to go to the Eagles and Dragons Publishing Patreon page to watch the introductory video and check out the patronage levels and exciting rewards.

https://www.patreon.com/EaglesandDragonsPublishing

Join us for an exciting future as we bring the past to life!

RESOURCES

There are many resources to be found online for researching, writing, publishing and marketing. The list below includes just a few that we have used and found helpful in our own writing and publishing journey. We hope you find them useful too…

Research

Translations of various sources are available for free on these sites:

- www.perseus.tufts.edu
- www.theoi.com
- www.gutenberg.org
- www.loebclassics.com (fee based)
- http://penelope.uchicago.edu/Thayer/E/Roman/Texts/home.html

Writing

Writing and e-book creation software for authors and publishers:

- Scrivener (https://www.literatureandlatte.com/scrivener/overview)
- Vellum (https://vellum.pub)

Books to inspire your writing and story creation:

- *The Hero with a Thousand Faces*, by Joseph Campbell
- *Joseph Campbell and the Power of Myth*, with Bill Moyers and Joseph Campbell
- *The Story Grid*, by Sean Coin
- *The War of Art*, by Steven Pressfield
- *Turning Pro*, by Steven Pressfield

Publishing

Books to help you publish your work traditionally:

- *Writer's Market*, by Writer's Digest Books
- *Guide to Literary Agents*, by Writer's Digest Books
- *Novel and Short Story Writer's Market*, by Writer's Digest Books

Sites to use when searching for literary agents and traditional publishers:

- Preditors and Editors (https://pred-ed.com/)
- Publishers Marketplace (https://www.publishersmarketplace.com)
- Publishers Weekly (https://www.publishersweekly.com)
- Writer Beware (https://www.sfwa.org/other-resources/for-authors/writer-beware/)

ISBN number information:

- International ISBN Agency (https://www.isbn-international.org)
- Bowker ISBN Agency (http://www.bowker.com/publishers)
- Library and Archives Canada (http://www.bac-lac.gc.ca/eng/services/isbn-canada/pages/isbn-canada.aspx) *Free ISBNs for Canadian authors and publishers only*

Publishing platforms:

- Amazon KDP (Kindle Direct Publishing on Amazon) (https://kdp.amazon.com/en_US/)

- Kobo Writing Life (https://www.kobo.com/us/en/p/writinglife)
- Apple Books (https://www.apple.com/itunes/working-itunes/sell-content/books/)
- Google Play Books (https://play.google.com/books/publish/)

Aggregator platforms to publish your book to all stores at once:

- Publish Drive (https://publishdrive.com)
- Draft2Digital (https://www.draft2digital.com)

Audio Book publishing platforms:

- ACX (for publishing to Amazon's Audible) (https://www.acx.com)
- Findaway Voices (https://findawayvoices.com)
- Kobo Writing Life (same link as above)

Online publishing courses:

- Mark Dawson's Self-Publishing 101

(https://learn.selfpublishingformula.com/p/101/)
- The Creative Penn Courses (https://www.thecreativepenn.com/courses/)

Marketing

Online courses to help with your marketing:

- The Creative Penn website building tutorial (https://www.thecreativepenn.com/authorwebsite/)
- Mark Dawson's Self-Publishing Formula (https://selfpublishingformula.com/start-here/)

Mailing list services:

- Mailchimp (https://mailchimp.com)
- ConvertKit (https://convertkit.com)
- Aweber (https://www.aweber.com)
- Mailerlite (https://www.mailerlite.com)

Book Publishing and Marketing Podcasts:

- The Creative Penn (https://www.thecreativepenn.com/podcasts/)
- The Sell More Books Show (http://sellmorebooksshow.com)

Book delivery platforms:

- BookFunnel (https://bookfunnel.com)

Direct sales platforms:

- Selz (https://selz.com)
- Payhip (https://payhip.com)

Image creation tools:

- Canva (https://www.canva.com)
- PIXLR (https://pixlr.com)

Crowdsourcing and patronage platforms:

- Patreon (https://www.patreon.com)
- Kickstarter (https://www.kickstarter.com)
- GoFundMe (https://www.gofundme.com)

There are no affiliate links in this book.

ABOUT THE AUTHOR

Adam Alexander Haviaras is a writer and historian who has studied ancient and medieval history and archaeology in Canada and the United Kingdom. He currently resides in Stratford, Ontario with his wife and children where he is continuing his research and writing other works of historical fantasy.

Historical Fiction/Fantasy Titles
The Eagles and Dragons Series

The Dragon: Genesis (Prequel)
A Dragon among the Eagles (Prequel)
Children of Apollo (Book I)
Killing the Hydra (Book II)
Warriors of Epona (Book III)
Isle of the Blessed (Book IV)
The Stolen Throne (Book V)
The Blood Road (Book VI)
The Eagles and Dragons Legionary Box Set (Books 0-I-II)

The Eagles and Dragons Tribune Box Set (Books III-IV-V)

The Carpathian Interlude Series

The Carpathian Interlude - Complete Trilogy Box Set
Immortui (Part I)
Lykoi (Part II)
Thanatos (Part III)

The Mythologia Series

Chariot of the Son
Wheels of Fate
A Song for the Underworld

Heart of Fire: A Novel of the Ancient Olympics

Saturnalia: A Tale of Wickedness and Redemption in Ancient Rome

Short Stories

The Sea Released
Theoi
Nex (or, The Warrior Named for Death)

Titles in the Historia Non-fiction Series

Historia I: Celtic Literary Archetypes in *The Mabinogion*: A Study of the Ancient Tale of *Pwyll, Lord of Dyved*

Historia II: Arthurian Romance and the Knightly Ideal: A study of Medieval Romantic Literature and its Effect upon Warrior Culture in Europe

Historia III: *Y Gododdin*: The Last Stand of Three Hundred Britons - Understanding People and Events during Britain's Heroic Age

Historia IV: Camelot: The Historical, Archaeological and Toponymic Considerations for South Cadbury Castle as King Arthur's Capital

Eagles and Dragons Publishing Guides

Writing the Past: The Eagles and Dragons Publishing Guide to Researching, Writing, Publishing and Marketing Historical Fiction and Historical Fantasy

To connect with Adam and learn more about the ancient world visit www.eaglesanddragonspublishing.com

Sign up for the Eagles and Dragons Publishing Newsletter at www.eaglesanddragonspublishing.com/newsletter-join-the-legions/ to receive a FREE BOOK, first access to new releases and posts on ancient history, special offers, and much more!

Readers can also connect with Adam on Twitter @AdamHaviaras and Instagram @ adam_haviaras.

On Facebook you can 'Like' the Eagles and Dragons page to get regular updates on new historical fiction and non-fiction from Eagles and Dragons Publishing.

www.ingramcontent.com/pod-product-compliance
Lightning Source LLC
Chambersburg PA
CBHW071428070526
44578CB00001B/37